THE TRUMP REVOLUTION

The Donald's Creative Destruction Deconstructed

BY ILANA MERCER

Politically Incorrect Press

Washington (USA)

All inquiries should be addressed to Politically Incorrect Press, P.O. Box 1770, Issaquah, WA 98027

Library of Congress Cataloging-in-Publication data
Mercer, Ilana
The Trump Revolution/by Ilana Mercer, 1st ed.
Includes select bibliography and index
ISBN: 978-0-9741039-1-4

1. Political Science—Political theory—Nationalism. Nation state. 2. Political Science—Political science—Consensus. Consent of the governed. 2. Political institutions and public administration (United States)—Political rights. Practical politics. 3. Political institutions and public administration (United States)—Political parties.

Library of Congress Control Number: 2016944519

Printed in the United States of America
Photography: Arlene Chambers

WHAT THE PEOPLE ARE SAYING

"I remember our exchanges [during the Iraq War], and I continue to enjoy your columns!"

~ **JIM WEBB**, former Democratic candidate for president, 2015, secretary of the navy, in the Reagan administration, Vietnam-War veteran, all-round Braveheart, recipient of the Navy Cross, the Silver Star Medal, two Bronze Star Medals and two Purple Hearts

"Ilana Mercer is no mere system-builder. Rather, it is an intense self-consciousness—of her views, yes, but, just as tellingly, of her life experiences—that accounts for Mercer's unrelenting pursuit of the logic of the paleolibertarian ideal: an ideal of liberty brought down from the clouds to the nit and the grit of the history and culture from which it emerged."

~ **JACK KERWICK, Ph.D.**, professor of philosophy, Rowan College, author, *The American Offensive: Dispatches From The Front*, columnist, Beliefnet.com, Town Hall

"Having read your columns throughout the years, I think I know you a little bit—I know you come from a very intellectual point of view, an intellectually honest point of view ..."

~ **SEAN HANNITY**, conservative political commentator, host of *Hannity* on Fox News & *The Sean Hannity Show*, nationally syndicated talk radio show

"Ilana Mercer is a remarkably gifted writer who deserves, and who I am sure will eventually receive, much wider recognition."

~ **DAVID CONWAY, Ph.D**., senior research fellow at CIVITAS, emeritus professor, Roehampton University, author, *Classical Liberalism: The Unvanquished Ideal*, *In Defence of the Realm: The Place of Nations in Classical Liberalism*, and many more

"All I can tell you is that you can't win an argument with this woman. I've tried and failed."

~ **VICTOR NIEDERHOFFER, Ph.D**., bestselling author, statistician, noted stock-market investor, polymath, founder of the *Objectivist*, New York City Junto liberty forum

"I consider Ilana Mercer a great mind."

~ **JAY TALYOR**, Austrian-perspective investor, banker and broadcaster, media commentator and hardcore gold bug

"I admire your individualism, you are patently not subject to 'group think'—all too increasingly rare nowadays."

~ **JAMES GRISHAM**, aka "Sweet Baby James," producer, *The Sean Hannity Show*

"Only a very few commentators, such as Antiwar.com's Justin Raimondo, Pat Buchanan and ILANA MERCER, can truly say that they were opposed from the start to the expensive, unconstitutional and ultimately useless abuses of the American military that have been inflicted upon it by Republican and Democratic commanders in chief over the last nine years."

~ **VOX DAY**, publisher, bad boy of science fiction, video game designer, author of *The Return of the Great Depression*

"Next to Rothbard, I believe you and Hans-Hermann Hoppe are the best libertarian writers I know of. I've read all your articles. I had been arguing with [certain libertarians] about immigration for months. You were the only person who challenged the libertarian establishment on immigration, and you were right."

~ **ML,** 10/8/2015

"I have been reading your articles since 2004 when I was in Iraq. Your wisdom and thinking have changed the way I look at the world."

~ **LEN C** ., "reader for life," written from Basra, Iraq

"Ilana Mercer is a true intellectual, and if human cloning were possible, an immediate requisition should be submitted to clone 100 copies of Ilana Mercer for a starter. Leftists rarely challenge her head-on since they rapidly discover all they have is a broken pencil when coming up against her powerful pen. Let's hope that God gives her many more years to use her powerful pen to fight for freedom."

~ **JACK KETTLER,** Amazon.com

"A towering intellect and a true stateswoman. The country could not do better than to choose you as its perpetual president and national treasure. Would that every citizen educated himself or herself as you have done and thought like you ..."

~ **DOUGLAS WELLS**, WND reader

"A sense of modesty and proper comportment may be keeping Ilana from stating the obvious. Since I have neither, I'll go ahead and say it; Mercer for Secretary of State! Her Cape Parrot would do a better job as press secretary than anyone in recent memory, so it's a twofer, like Bill and Hill without the speaker fees! Seriously, I seem to recall that Ilana was an informal advisor to the last Ron Paul campaign and has a good outsider's eye for the absurdities of the current political situation and actors; she knows the neocons cold and isn't afraid to call them out. Donald needs to get her on the horn, stat."

~ **JEFF ALBERTSON**, The Unz Review, March 20, 2016

"A good, clear thinker who brilliantly sets out on paper that which she considers important enough to write about. Her paragraphs arrive randomly sprinkled with wit, wisdom and tragedy. She seldom repeats herself or attempts to impress the reader by churning out a shedload of boring facts—which we can all, in any event, find out for ourselves should we feel the need to. Ilana not only owns the sort of retentive ability that bestows her with great confidence, she also demonstrates a fertile and often delightfully wicked imagination. I've found a diamond."

~ **JOHN WARREN,** UK Libertarian Alliance, December 13, 2015

BOOKS BY ILANA MERCER

Into The Cannibal's Pot: Lessons For America From Post-Apartheid South Africa

Broad Sides: One Woman's Clash With A Corrupt Culture

With thanks to Sean Mercer & Tom
Flood for making this possible

CONTENTS

Opening Statement: Welcome To The Post-Constitutional Jungle
1

The Bureaucratic Complex 11

The Conservative Complex 12

The Party Complex 19

The Media Complex 22

Morning In American? No. But Merry Christmas Will Do Just Fine 28

No Political Criminal Record 29

Corruption Codified In Law 33

The Scarlet Letter 'E' 39

A Love For The People 41

1. A Candidate To 'Kick The Crap Out Of All The Politicians' 44

2. No Trump Apology Tour 49

3. Does Mccain Owe Mea Culpa To POWS And Men Missing In Action? 53

4. Trump Should Triangulate 59

Political Power Vs. Economic Power 59

Raping Reality With Political Theory 61

Party Pooper 63

Noblesse Oblige 64

5. Trump Could Send The System's Sycophants Scattering 66

6. The Golden Goose That Henpecked Donald Trump 70

7. Trump's Reaganesque Mic Moment 75

Contents

8. Trump's Good For The English Language   79

When In The U.S. Or Britain, Speak English.   79

Restoring Truth To Language   80

9. Donald, Don't Let Fox News Roger America ... Again   84

10. A Halloween Horror Story In The People's House   90

11. What Trump's Up Against: In The West, The Inmates Run The Asylum   96

12. Reducing Murder-By-Muslim In The Homeland   101

The Collateral-Damage Calculus   102

Squandering Vs. Conserving Scarce Resources   104

In Politics, 'Nothing Succeeds Like Failure'   106

13. Neutralizing Neoconservative War Tourette's   107

14. Trump's Invisible, Poor White Army's Waiting On The Ropes   113

15. Trump's Promise To Nullify Laws   118

16. The Me-Myself-And-I Megyn Production Messes With Trump   126

17. The Winning Trump Ticket And Cabinet   134

18. The Murdoch Media: Root 'N Branch For Marcobot   140

19. Making America Great Means Taking Down 'W'   146

20. Trump Called Bush A Liar & Won South Carolina (Nevada, Too)   151

21. Trump Nation Sick 'N Tired Of Racial Sadomasochism   157

22. Trump And Trade   162

23. Trump Doesn't Need To Talk Like A Conservative   167

24. Wrong, Donald Trump, Islam Loves Us ... To Bits   174

The Trump Revolution

25. April Fields' Day: Michelle Fool & Journalism's Feminization
180

26. Trump Vs. The Banana Republicans 184

27. Trump's America First Policy: Remarkably Sophisticated 189

28. Someone Should Tell Bill Kristol Dwarf Tossing Is Cruel 195

29. Testosterone, Going, Going, Almost Gone ... 199

Mighty Mouse 200

Don't Do The Thymus Thump 202

Anger-Shaming 204

The Inevitability Of Eternal Verities, Even Biology 205

Socio-Chemical Castration 209

Dissolving 'The Constitution Of Man' In The Service Of Sameness 210

Closing Argument: The Power Tools Of An Illiberal Politics 213

Time's Buy Direct Revolution 219

No To Neoconservatism 220

Paul Ryan, Another Guy Who Never Built A Thing 224

Yes To Natural Justice 225

A Concurrent Majority Rising? 226

Justice's Jaws of Life 231

Recrudescence Of An Older Right 234

Select Bibliography 236

Index 239

Biographical Note: On Patriotism 249

OPENING STATEMENT: WELCOME TO THE POST-CONSTITUTIONAL JUNGLE

Donald J. Trump is smashing an enmeshed political spoils system to bits: the media complex, the political and party complex, the conservative poseur complex. In the age of unconstitutional government—Democratic and Republican—this process of creative destruction can only increase the freedom quotient.

We inhabit what broadcaster Mark Levin has termed a post-constitutional America. The libertarian ideal—where the chains that tether us to an increasingly tyrannical national government are loosened and power is devolved once again to the smaller units of society—is a long way away.

In this post-constitutional jungle, the law of the jungle prevails. In this legislative jungle, the options are few: Do Americans get a benevolent authoritarian to undo the legacies of Barack Obama, George W. Bush and those who went before? Or, does the ill-defined entity called The People continue to submit to Demopublican diktats, past and present?

Until such time when the individual is king again, and a decentralized constitution that guarantees regional and individual autonomy has been restored—the process of creative destruction begun by Donald Trump is likely the best Americans can hope for. Thus the endorsement over these pages is not necessarily for the policies of Trump, but for The Process of Trump.

In the age of unconstitutional government—Democratic and Republican—the best liberty lovers can look to is action and counteraction, force and counterforce in the service of liberty.

And a force of nature Mr. Trump most certainly is. You name it; Trump is tossing and goring it. The well-oiled elements that sustain and make the American political system cohere are suddenly in Brownian motion, oscillating like never before. An entrenched punditocracy, a self-anointed, meritless intelligentsia (which is not very intelligent and draws its financial sustenance from the political spoils system), oleaginous politicians, slick media, big money: They've all worked in tandem to advance a grand government—national and transnational—that aggrandizes its constituent elements, while diminishing those it's supposed to serve. These political players have built the den of iniquity Trump is destroying.

Against these forces—RNC, NRO, NATO, a whole alphabet soup of acronyms—*is Trump, acting as a political Samson that threatens to bring the den of iniquity crashing down on its patrons.*

Trump has the necessary moxie to blast away at an overweening political system. He has already done a laudable job of fumigating some serious snake pits. By drastically weakening these links—diminishing The Machine's moving parts—Trump might just help loosen the chains that bind the individual to central government, national and transnational.

Undeterred, the Trump holy terror has even blasted the scold from Fort Vatican for living walled-off in Vatican City, while preaching to Americans that for their security needs, they must reject walls and "build bridges." Pope Francis' shopworn shibboleths, disgorged by Hillary Clinton too, are straight out of a Chinese, fortune-cookie wrapper.

Trump has also begun to question NATO, a noose around the American people's neck. By so doing, rejoices Justin Raimondo of Antiwar.com, Trump is "repudiating the entire framework of U.S. foreign policy since 1947." "He's confronting the post-WWII international order—and winning."

The North Atlantic Treaty Organization is bad for those who must sponsor it and live with its policies in perpetuity; it's good for the sinecured politicians and functionaries who feed upon it. These special interests have negotiated Empire for themselves; a mess of pottage for The People. Of the American industrial base only a husk remains. Rails Raimondo:

> [T]he Japanese don't have to worry about defending themselves and they also get the economic benefits of having a strictly protected market while they hollow out our industrial base with cheap cars and precision machinery. This is the price we pay for the American empire – an imperium, as the Old Right writer and editor

Garet Garrett put it many years ago, 'where everything goes out and nothing comes in.'

You could say Trump is coming from a libertarian angle: Government lives off the people. Government must, at the very least, work for the people. More laudably, Trump doesn't collapse the distinction between "America" and the U.S. government.

To Trump, making America great means making the people great.

Trump exhibits no confusion of category. He doesn't equate "America" with the U.S. government. To the political cast, conversely, "America" is the U.S. government. To them, making America great means making government great.

Understandably, The Donald has the political players rising on their hind legs in defense of their realm. And he is shattering the totems and taboos these players enforce. Debated as never before are vexations like immigration, Islam and, yes, the legitimacy of the Republican National Committee.

In a country whose self-anointed *cognoscenti* suffer infectious, historic Alzheimer's, *The Trump Revolution* does the job of, first, chronicling and deconstructing the manner in which a political *tabula rasa*, Trump, took a wrecking ball to barriers erected by cultural Marxists by any other name—barrier that proscribe open, honest discussion on the defining issues of the day.

Opening Statement: Welcome To The Post-Constitutional Jungle

The quintessential post-constitutional candidate, Trump's candidacy is for the age when the Constitution itself is unconstitutional. Like it or not, the original Constitution is a dead letter. The natural- and common law traditions, once loadstars for lawmakers, have been buried under the rubble of legislation and statute. However much one shovels the muck of lawmaking aside, natural justice and the Founders' original intent remain buried too deep to exhume.

Consider: America's Constitution makers bequeathed a central government of delegated and enumerated powers. The Constitution gives Congress only some eighteen specific legislative powers. Nowhere among these powers is Social Security, civil rights (predicated as they are on grotesque violations of property rights), Medicare, Medicaid, and the elaborate public works sprung from the General Welfare and Interstate Commerce Clauses.

There is simply no warrant in the Constitution for most of what the Federal Frankenstein does.

The welfare clause stipulates that "Congress will have the power … to provide for the general welfare." And even though the general clause is followed by a detailed enumeration of the limited powers so delegated; our overlords, over decades of *dirigisme*, have taken Article I, Section 8 to mean that government can pick The People's pockets and proceed with force against them for any perceivable purpose and project.

For another example of the endemic usurpation of The People, rendering the original Constitutional scheme obsolete, take the work of the generic jury. With his description of the relationship between jury and people, American scholar of liberty Lysander Spooner conjures evocative imagery. A jury is akin to the "body of the people." Trial by jury is the closest thing to a trial by the whole country. Yet courts in the nation's centralized court system, the Supreme Court included, regularly disregard and replace a jury's verdict with a manufactured national consensus.

Courts are in the business of harmonizing law across the nation, rather than allowing communities to live under laws they author, as guaranteed by The Tenth Amendment to the Constitution:

The powers not delegated to the United States by the Constitution, nor prohibited by it to the States, are reserved to the States respectively, or to the people.

In American federalism, the rights of the individual are secured through strict limits imposed on the power of the central government by a Bill of Rights and the division of authority between autonomous states and a federal government. Like juries, states had been entrusted with the power to beat back the federal occupier and void unconstitutional federal laws. States' rights are "an essential Americanism," wrote Old Rightist Frank Chodorov. The Founding Fathers as well as the opponents of the Constitution agreed on the principle of divided authority as a safeguard to the rights of the individual."

Duly, Thomas Jefferson and James Madison perfected a certain doctrine in the Virginia and Kentucky Resolutions of

Opening Statement: Welcome To The Post-Constitutional Jungle

1798. "The Virginia Resolutions," explains historian Thomas E. Woods, Jr., "spoke of the states' rights to 'interpose' between the federal government and the people of the states; the Kentucky Resolutions used the term nullification—the states, they said, could nullify federal laws that they believed to be unconstitutional." Jefferson," emphasizes Woods, "considered states' rights a much more important and effective safeguard of people's liberties than the 'checks and balances' among the three branches of the federal government."

And for good reason. While judicial review was intended to curb Congress and restrain the executive, in reality, the unholy judicial, legislative and executive federal trinity has simply colluded in an alliance that has helped to abolish the Tenth Amendment.

And how well has First-Amendment jurisprudence served our constitutionalists? Establishment-clause cases are a confusing and capricious legal penumbra. Sometimes displays of the Hebraic Decalogue are taken to constitute the establishment of a state religion. Other times not. This body of law forever teeters on conflating the injunction against the establishment of a state religion with an injunction against the expression of faith—especially discriminating against the founding faith in taxpayer-supported spaces. The end result has been the expulsion of religion from the public square and the suppression therein of freedom of religion.

On the topic of religious freedom, Jefferson was prolific, too. The Virginia Statute for Religious Freedom was a crowning achievement for which he wished to be remembered, along with the Declaration of Independence and the founding of the University of Virginia.

With "Congress shall make no law respecting the establishment of religion, or prohibiting the exercise thereof," Jefferson intended, confirms David N. Meyer, author of *Jefferson's Constitutional Thought*, to guarantee both "an absolute free exercise of religion and an absolute prohibition of an establishment of religion."

Yet somehow, the kind of constitutional thought that carries legal sway today prohibits expressions of faith or displays of a civilizing moral code in government controlled spheres. Given our view of government's immoral *modus operandi*, we libertarians find this amusingly apropos. But this is not what Jefferson had in mind for early Americans.

Indeed, why would anyone, bar the ACLU, object to "thou shall not kill" or "thou shall not commit adultery, steal or covet?" The Ten Commandments can hardly be perceived as an instrument for state proselytization. Nevertheless, the law often takes displays of the Decalogue on tax-payer funded property as an establishment of a state religion.

"I consider the government of the U.S. as interdicted by the Constitution from intermeddling with religious institutions, their doctrines, discipline, or exercise," Jefferson expatiated. He then gets to the soul of the subject: "This results not only from the provision that no law shall be made respecting the establishment, or free exercise of religion but also from the Tenth Amendment, which reserves to the states [or to the people] the powers not delegated to the U.S."

However, not even conservative constitutional originalists are willing to concede that the Fourteenth Amendment and the attendant Incorporation Doctrine have obliterated the Constitution's federal scheme, as expressed in the once-impregnable Tenth Amendment.

What does this mean?

You know the drill, but are always surprised anew by it. Voters pass a law under which a plurality wishes to live. Along comes a U.S. district judge and voids the law, citing a violation of the Fourteenth Amendment's Equal Protection Clause.

Voters elect to prohibit government from sanctioning gay marriage. A U.S. district judge voids voter-approved law for violating the Fourteenth Amendment's Equal Protection Clause. These periodical contretemps around gay marriage are perfectly proper judicial activism heralded by the Fourteenth Amendment. Yet not even conservative constitutional originalists are willing to cop to the propriety of it all. If the Bill of Rights was intended to place strict limits on federal power and protect individual and locality from the national government—the Fourteenth Amendment effectively defeated that purpose by placing the power to enforce the Bill of Rights in federal hands, where it was never intended to be. Put differently, matters previously subject to state jurisdiction have been pulled into the orbit of a judiciary.

The gist of it: Jeffersonian constitutional thought is no longer in the Constitution; its revival unlikely.

As ardent a defender of the Constitution as constitutional scholar James McClellan was—even he conceded, sadly, that the Constitution makers were mistaken to rely on the good faith of Congress and their observance of the requirements of liberty, to reign in an Über-Presidency in the making, and prevent the rise of a legislating bureaucracy and an overweening judiciary—a judiciary of scurrilous statists that has, of late, found in the Constitution a mandate to compel commerce by forcing individual Americans to purchase health insurance on pains of a fine.

John G. Roberts Jr., chief of our country's legal politburo of proctologists, rewrote Barack Obama's Affordable Care Act, and then proceeded to provide the fifth vote to uphold the individual mandate undergirding the law, thereby undeniably and obscenely extending Congress's taxing power.

"[B]uried in the constitutional thickets" are "huge presidential powers," conceded historian Paul Johnson, in his *History of the American People*. The American president "was much stronger than most kings of the day, rivaled or exceeded only by the 'Great Autocrat,' the Tsar of Russia (and in practice stronger than most tsars). These powers were not explored until Andrew Jackson's time, half a century on, when they astonished and frightened many people."

The lying words of the Republican presidential candidates notwithstanding—for most promise constitutionalism—a liberty-lover's best hope is to see the legacy of the dictator who went before overturned for a period of time.

The toss-up in the 2016 election is, therefore, between submitting to the Democrats' war on whites, the wealthy and Wal-Mart, or being bedeviled by the Republicans' wars on the world: Russia, China, Assad and The Ayatollahs. Or, suffering all the indignities listed and more if Candidate Clinton is victorious.

The modest hope here is that an utterly different political animal, Donald Trump, might actually do some good for the countrymen he genuinely seems to love.

The Bureaucratic Complex

To Roberts was posed, in September of 2005, the mother of all confirmation questions. Out of the blue, some senator, whose name I can't recall, asked Roberts whether the Administrative State against which Americans struggle was compatible with the Constitution and the Founding Founders' vision. The Managerial State—its endless rules and regulations—whence does it derive its legitimacy? Roberts answered what was a philosophical question with a legalistic ramble about administrative law.

It wasn't that Roberts was flummoxed by this First-Principles quandary out of the Senate; it just seemed alien to him; it swooshed right by.

The bureaucratic complex denotes the federal bureaucracy, aka "the Secret State"; the thing James Burnham called The Managerial State. It has been imbued with ever-accreting, extraconstitutional powers. In the modern Managerial State that is America; citizens live and labor under rules and regulations set by bureaucrats and social engineers, who've been deputized to wield enormous discretionary powers. This Monster State is incompatible with what the Constitution and the Founding Founders bequeathed. If indeed Mr. Trump is able to replace this self-directing state-within-a-state with his own private-sector high-performers, perhaps even curtail the reach of public administration, it's worth a shot.

The Conservative Complex

The intellectual custodians of conservatism have hoisted their epistolary pitchforks against Trump. "Conservatives Against Trump" is also the title of a *National Review* (NR) January 2016 issue, in which NR galvanized "bravely" against the Republican base rising, as represented by the anti-establishment candidates.

"Prominent conservatives" or "leading conservatives" is how the *National Review* peanut gallery has been anointed by the menagerie of morons that is the American media. But most of the *National Review* recruits to have enlisted against Trump are conservatives in name only.

Jack Kerwick, a columnist whose métier is the philosophy of conservatism, has argued that the absence in

their collective works of a hint of the conservatism of
founding philosophers Edmund Burke, "the patron saint" of
conservatism," his "20th century's American reincarnation,
Russell Kirk," even Michael Oakeshott—renders the
conservative provenance of the National Reviewniks
dubious at best.

In particular, that *National Review*'s promotion of
"'American Exceptionalism,'" the radically ahistorical
doctrine that America is not a historically and culturally-
specific country but an 'idea,' an abstract 'proposition'"—
makes this lot out-and-out unconservative.

Whereas the National Reviewniks constantly yack it up
for a global, ideological American Manifest Destiny; the
conservatism of Kirk and Burke was rooted in an allegiance
to and love of the "little platoons" of one's country; what
Burke described as a man's social mainstay—his family,
friends, coreligionists, coworkers.

One might say *National Review* stands athwart historic
conservatism, to borrow from magazine founder William F.
Buckley's famous mission statement to stand athwart
history.

Into this ongoing, historic fray stepped Dr. Paul
Gottfried and his 2007 book, *Conservatism in America: Making
Sense of the American Right*. Gottfried was a personal friend to
Kirk. He is described in a new, 2016, Kirk biography as his
"political ally in the Sisyphean task of opposing the (probably
inevitable) neoconservative takeover of Conservatism Inc."
"Kirk," laments Gottfried, in an Unz Review essay, "was
considered the leading thinker of the American Right." His

"thought was infinitely more sophisticated, and insightful, than anything coming out of the official Conservative Movement." Russell Kirk has, however, been usurped by lightweights like Jonah Goldberg.

Rooted as it was in the "classical conservative legacy," Kirk's work was antithetical to *National Review's* neoconservative program of using "political ideology as a substitute for traditional organic ties." Kirk's conservative version of the good society was "aligned with early nineteenth-century classical conservatism," contends Gottfried. His "defense of social hierarchy" and "revulsion for all efforts at homogenizing human societies" doesn't fit with the Beltway's radical egalitarianism, left and "right." Spreading "human rights" to the entire human race would have made Kirk cringe.

Be it reflexive or deliberate, the *modus operandi* of this relatively new American establishment Right is clear. While its "affluent spokesmen" diligently keep up "the partisan tone of debate," they toil frenetically to "accommodate talking partners on the Left-Center." To smooth rough edges," conservatives will always opt to "marginalize their own right wing," and "distance themselves from those who seem more conservative in their principles than the goal of bridge–building might render acceptable." According to Gottfried:

> Mainstream conservatives, especially those identified with foundations, have pursued this course not only to reassure liberal media

colleagues but to improve their place in the Republican Party.

Indeed, there's an undeniable and comfortable convergence between the two political parties and their attendant factions. Republicans and movement conservatives are now part of the smart set. So it is that "conservatives continue to appease and appeal to media talking partners," "to find common purpose with the liberal establishment," to "avoid any appearance of what the Left would regard as extremism." The strategy under discussion is informed by an appeal to "permanent values." Such appeals, especially in a movement that lacks historic continuity, serve to create a false sense of permanence (as do they serve to enforce ideological conformity, as this writer observes in Chapter 21). Creating a sense of permanence conceals the conservative movement's "general tendency to move leftwards to accommodate those with whom it shares the public spotlight." More crucially, argues Gottfried, the values veneer compensates for "a lack of connection to an older and more genuine conservatism."

Especially rich in this context is the accusation leveled at Trump by the "conservative" camp that he has orchestrated a hostile takeover of conservatism. The "American establishment Right" is itself a product of a hostile takeover of the American Old Right, which had held to classical liberalism and strict constitutionalism. The current iteration of the conservative movement is a result of a hostile takeover, in the 1980s, by neoconservatives, many of them repentant Communists. "Taft Republicans, anti-New Deal Buckleyites of the 1950s, southern agrarians and American isolationists: These "organic strains of [American] conservatism" were usurped by neoconservatives.

The "post war conservative movement," as expressed in the "present media think tank" structures, is an artificial movement whose unity and support derive partly from "manufacturing values" and "imposing solidarity." The manner in which neoconservatives come down hard on dissenters, not excluding the perennial purge, is yet another by-product of this ideological kudzu.

It is no coincidence that Conservatism Inc. has spent decades lunging leftwards, appealing to egalitarian ideals, adapting to a "highly centralized public administration," militantly promoting a "neo-Wilsonian foreign policy," and affirming the American State at every turn, in its pursuit of values-based, often manifestly cooked-up wars. As Gottfried sees it, the neoconservative American State is comparable in its philosophical impetus to the "leviathan state of the French Revolution." In practice, the big conservative cheeses evince less of an attachment to the American heritage than to the Jacobin tradition—expressed in a powerful, centralized, universalist state that aggrandizes abstractions and subordinates communities to a national general will.

As I see it, our neoconservative pseudo-conservatives speak like Tocqueville but act like Robespierre.

The organization that "crystalized" around Buckley in 1955 included many a "recovering Marxist" who now wished to direct the movement's efforts at fighting Communism around the world. The "dismantling of the welfare state" would soon become secondary to waging war.

The hangover from this mindset, circa 2016, is that "restraining the reach of the central government" is very much incidental and separate (in, say, neoconservative Marco Rubio's thinking) to putting Putin in his place, removing Bashar Assad, and continuing to facilitate those plant-based, color-coded revolutions around the world: Purple in Iraq, Blue in Kuwait, Cotton in Uzbekistan, Grape in Moldova, Orange in the Ukraine, Rose in Georgia, Tulip in Kyrgizstan, Cedar in Lebanon, Jasmine in Tunisia, Green in Iran, still un-christened in Russia and Syria.

By dismissing Mr. Trump's vast constituency, the "Against Trump" *faux* conservatives at *National Review* are certainly purging a considerable number of American populists—this as the same group continues to make overtures to the Left, not least in embracing their version of history, *herstory* and history-from-below.

There were many reasons not racist for which to dislike Martin Luther King Jr., as the Old Right did. "Terrible," "tricky" and "a phony" is how MLK was described by the nation's most engaging first lady, Democrat Jacqueline Kennedy. "His associations with communists" is why Jackie's husband ordered the wiretaps on King. Mrs. Kennedy's brother-in-law, Robert Kennedy—recounts Patrick J. Buchanan in *Suicide of a Superpower*—"saw to it that the FBI carried out the order." Among his other endearing qualities, Martin Luther King Jr. had "declared that the Goldwater campaign bore dangerous signs of Hitlerism." Indisputably, MLK set the tone for "assailing America as irredeemably racist" forever after. Other brothers have built on MLK's work to sculpt careers as professional race hustlers.

Faithful to this legacy, the New Right now counts among its greatest heroes not only MLK, but the minor abolitionist Harriet Tubman. Major abolitionist and murderer John Brown is close to making the cut, at least in the eyes of *National Review's* Kevin D. Williamson. Williamson "reached peak leftism" when he declared his sympathies were "more with John Brown than John Calhoun," in an article titled "We Have Officially Reached Peak Leftism" (June 24, 2015). In 1856, Brown's free-soil activists snatched five pro-slavery settlers near Pottawatomie Creek, Kansas and split the captives' skulls with broadswords, in an act of biblical retribution gone mad. Still more problematic is *National Review's* new-found tolerance for journalism favorable to the barbarism of Communist leader Leon Trotsky. In the June 3, 2003 issue, recounts Gottfried, contributor Stephen Schwartz held up "Trotsky for special commendation." Fast forward to March 2, 2016, and neoconservative historian Max Boot is stumping for Stalin: "I would sooner vote for Josef Stalin than I would vote for Donald Trump," Boot told the *New York Times*.

As to the mantle of "thinkers" conferred upon the "Against Trump" lot by an unthinking media: Kenneth Minogue was a "thinker." Roger Scruton is a thinker. John O'Sullivan can think (which is probably why he was nudged out as editor of *National Review*, in favor of intellectual pygmy Rich Lowery). But Mona Charen? She's a mediocre scribbler, at best. Dana Loesch is a gorgeous gun-toting broadcaster, Katie Pavlich youthful nullity, Glenn Beck an irrational mystic, Michael Mukasey a government functionary-cum-attorney and Jeb Bush cheerleader.

Thinkers? I don't think so.

In pondering the quality of the conservative brain trust, ask yourself this: Where's Chucky Krauthammer in the "Conservatives Against Trump" production? The ponderous, self-important neoconservative is nothing if not smart. He, too, is hopping mad over Trump. Why is Chucky nowhere to be found among those aligned "Against Trump" at *National Review?* My own working hypothesis is this: Krauthammer is not as stupid as the "Conservatives against Trump." For to come out as a collective in an attempt to overthrow a candidate so popular with the Republican base and beyond, as Trump is, is pretty stupid.

The Party Complex

The "Conservatives Against Trump" *National Review* flurry had been preceded by the "Stop Trump" convention, courtesy of Reince Priebus, chairman of the Republican National Committee. As detailed in "A Halloween Horror Story In The People's House" (Chapter 10), The House, dominated by Republicans, is the central node in a network that specializes in thwarting the electorate. And these Grand Old Party grandees are squirming. So furious has the GOP apparatus become for its failure to frustrate the will of grassroots Republicans—that Republican kingmakers and monied interests convened, late in November of 2015, at the Hotel Bel-Air in Los Angeles, to pledge possible support for ... Democrat Hillary Clinton!

"GOP donors want a puppet that they can control, and Donald Trump will never be that person," countered Trump's campaign manager. The next low to which our crypto-leftists stooped: Stop a Trump nomination by plotting a procedural sleight of hand—a brokered convention—warranted only when a candidate fails to secure the most delegates in the primaries. Threat of a contested convention is an acid test of sorts: When in December of 2015 good guy Ben Carson got wind of the Republican Party's scheme for such a convention, in the year ahead, he was scandalized, condemning "the GOP heads ... for trying to 'manipulate' the primary outcome." Carson has persists in his ethical position.

Conversely, when weak, whiny, insider John Kasich heard he might be the Anointed One at this very convention, chosen by Republican Party operatives to steal the nomination from Donald Trump, the governor rejoiced.

Inescapably obvious is that due to The Donald, the RNC is being exposed like never before for steering elections; it's being exposed as a central command that writes and rigs the rules of the political process. *A party the people increasingly hate is attempting to nominate presidential candidates the people haven't voted for.* So while Trump was winning over voters fair-and-square; Senator Ted Cruz had been notching "voterless victories" to his name. Cruz might not be a natural-born American citizen but he's proving to be a natural-born crook. Where state parties have been able to bypass the voters, cancel primaries and caucuses and award delegates at state conventions—Cruz and his crew swooped down to vacuum-up these delegates. In North Dakota, Colorado, Wyoming, even Georgia, where Trump won a primary, Cruz, posing as an "outsider," showed himself curiously comfortable with chalking up empty procedural wins. And while the senator from Texas waded into these polluted waters; Trump expressed disgust at being compelled to "buy" delegates:

> You're basically buying these people. You're basically saying, 'Delegate, listen, we're going to send you to Mar-a-Lago on a Boeing 757, you're going to use the spa, you're going to this, you're going to that, we want your vote.' That's a corrupt system.

Certainly when it comes to libertarian candidates, the RNC has behaved shoddily. With Trump's assist, early on in the cycle, the Republican campaigns revolted against Party tools who'd hitherto been bad-faith brokers between the public and any libertarian or constitutionally minded Republican candidate. It may not be much, but a battle is underway to decentralize and deregulate Republican politics. This struggle has failed to animate the obedient, authoritarian Left, which, by a great irony, refuses to protest the concentration of power in the grubby paws of Representative Debbie Wasserman Schultz, chair of the Democratic National Committee (DNC). Liberals, who are forever boasting about their radicalism and their rebellion against stagnant political strictures, are now criticizing the wonderful chaos in the GOP ranks. Like Trump, Bernie Sanders has appealed to his restive base over the heads of the DNC. Alas, the populist Left's favorite son has been sidelined by similar forces, not least the superdelegate subterfuge, where Party Bosses such as President Obama, Vice President Biden, former President Bill Clinton and his vice president, Al Gore—superdelegates all—get to tip the scales of justice.

As Sanders began eating into Clinton's lead, mid-April, the pundits intensified their incongruous prognostications: "Bernie can't possibly win." Mocked Mr. Trump: "Why can't Sanders win when he wins all the time?"

It's all in the system.

The Media Complex

Not enough can be said about the manner in which Mr. Trump has unseated the smug, crooked media organ sending it into a nose dive. The idiot's lantern, in particular, is monopolized by men and women who're of The system and for The System. Any wonder, then, that these traditional powerbrokers are bucking the thing that threatens their viability? Trump is getting an atrophied political system to oscillate. The particles hate him for it.

Opening Statement: Welcome To The Post-Constitutional Jungle

Like CNN and MSNBC, *National Journal* was—still is—hoping against hope that American voters would follow the lead of Macy's, NBC, Univision and Dubai, and ditch The Donald.

For dismissing the political staying power of Donald Trump, MSNBC attempted a token *mea culpa*, in the waning days of 2015, for themselves and their brethren throughout the malfunctioning media. However, whether they're missing the Trump phenom or the *casus belli* for war in Iraq—America's deeply stupid, self-anointed *cognoscenti* recognize truth only once card-carrying members arrive at it independently, grasp and broadcast it, sometimes years too late. Not so the marginalized writers of America. Not in 2012, but in 2002 did we pinpoint the wrongness of the Iraq War. And not in 2016, but on July 19, 2015—when this chronicle began—did some of us, not fortuitously, finger Trump as "a candidate to 'kick the crap out of all the politicians'" and "send the system's sycophants scattering" (August 14, 2015). His appeal, as this writer has contended since late in 2015, transcends left and right. Conversely, vaunted statistician Nate Silver "calculated, last November, that Trump's support was 'about the same share of people who think the Apollo moon landings were faked.'" (Professor Tyler Cowen of George Mason University properly downgraded wonder boy Silver's intellectual prowess. His prose was a sprawl that "evinces a greater affiliation to rigor with data analysis than to rigor with philosophy of science or for that matter rigor with rhetoric," wrote the good teacher.)

Naturally, or *natürlich*, *Time* magazine chose a kindred spirit as its person of the year, instead of the newsmaker of the year 2015. German Chancellors Angela Merkel was nominated for compelling Germans to shed an "old and haunting national identity" in favor of the Bismarckian Superstate that is the European Eurocracy. If *Time* is a dishonest broker in the news business, the special-needs media were likewise six months late to recognize the Trump revolution—and, in fact, still parade on piss-poor television panels raging against the reality of Trump. Thus did a Jeb Bush sycophant with a gig on CNN declare herself still in the denial stage of grief over Trump's ascent. Joined by the aforementioned Ana Navarro was S.E. Cupp, white-noise maker and colossal bore. This card-carrying member of the Republican Idiocracy had predicted a shoo-in for Jeb Bush. Now Cupp was threatening to sit out the election if she could not have her way. For the sake of her kids, she puffed sanctimoniously.

Helmed by fellow Canadian David Frum, the august *Atlantic* has inched closer to what I believe to be the political truth about Trump and his supporters. Frum's wide-ranging, thorough analysis was encapsulated in a piece titled: "The Great Republican Revolt: The GOP planned a dynastic restoration in 2016. Instead, it triggered an internal class war. Can the party reconcile the demands of its donors with the interests of its rank and file?" Alas, the central conceit that currently defines media, the writer of *The Atlantic* article included, is this: While The Right is always more courageous in bucking authority, the Trump revolt is not exclusively a Republican revolt. As I pointed out last year (Chapter 14), I get the distinct impression that the Trump revolution encompasses left and right; Republican, Democrat, Independent. And I don't believe I'm wrong. Certainly, as admitted in *The Atlantic*, the polls are underestimating Trump's support. The slow kids of media have discovered the methodological flaws inherent in survey methodology: Subjects are more likely to own-up to their political proclivities in anonymous, online surveys than in face-to-face or telephonic questionnaires.

The role of media is to report the news, not engage in activism. Yet news outlets led and misled with an "angle," or with their own aspirations, not with the reality on the ground, namely, the news. To wit, Donald Trump drew half the town of Biloxi, Mississippi, to a rally on January 2, 2016. Having abnegated their mandate to report on events, the malfunctioning media chose, on that occasion, to harp on why Islamic State preferred Hillary Clinton to Trump (by which they meant, presumably, to suggest Mr. Clinton would be a better fit for the role of president of the United States).

At the time of writing, Trump is holding three to four rallies a week, sometimes two a day; a day before and after a debate. To watch these events is to observe A Man of The People. Yet media is showing none of The Love. Befitting the lack of candid coverage, Trump began a campaign rally in Pensacola, Florida (January 13), by berating cameramen for refusing to pan out and capture the historic crowds that had assembled in the 10,000-capacity arena. Five thousand supporters were rumored to have been turned away. Also at the time of writing, media seem to have reflexively colluded to curtail coverage of Trump's inspiring events. Perhaps the networks ought to be busted for collusion under anti-Trust legislation? True libertarians abhor anti-Trust legislation and prosecution, but, as I said, *we're down to action and counteraction, force and counterforce in the service of liberty.*

So it was that neoconservative pundit Jonah Goldberg accused Americans of throwing a tantrum at establishment politicians and pundits. The word "tantrum" is meant to demean; it implies a hissy fit; a childish outburst of rage. As intent on quelling the rebellion against their establishment, GOP Media marionettes George Will and Michael Gerson, of "The Washington Post Conservative Club," dubbed Trump followers "xenophobic" like "a European right-wing party, a UKIP or a National Front in France," when, as patriot Pat Buchanan observed, on August 14, 2015:

> Both [those parties] arose to recapture the lost independence and sovereignty of their nations from the nameless, faceless bureaucrats of Brussels, those EU hacks who now dictate the kinds of laws and societies the Brits and French are permitted to have.

So the Media Complex brought in "The Kochtopus." Fox News Channel's Megyn Kelly was first to galvanize the Koch Brothers, the Grand Old Party's big guns, in her quasi-personal crusade against the anti-establishment

Republican candidate. The Trump guy was doing something right if he had angered the Koch kingmakers. Hard on Kelly's stilettoes was the *War Street Journal* (not a typo), featuring an article in which Koch complained about Trump (complaints later repeated to *Vanity Fair*, Megyn's *alma mater*). Trump had the WSJ fulminating. The neoconservative mouthpiece had declared that by attacking McMussolini (Senator John McCain), Donald Trump had finally crossed some uncrossable threshold and was destined to self-destruct. The hope-filled, unhinged sentiment was just that. The people have no particular love for Mr. McCain. Veterans soon got over Donald's diss.

"Talk to the hand," the American people seem to be telling the media establishment.

"In a Republican presidential field rich with esteemed governors and senators, tough-talking businessman Trump has managed to rise in the polls to be a top-tier candidate," grumbled one Lauren Fox. As Trump's popularity continued its precipitous climb, Senator Lindsey Graham (at a steady zero percent) maintained his lead with the news networks right until he quit the race. With the usual gall, the sophisticates at *The Atlantic* chalked up the Trump phenomenon to a lack of education among working- and middle-class voters. As always, Pat Buchanan regaled with a retort:

> Like The Donald, the American people are telling the establishment what Oliver Cromwell told the Rump Parliament, paraphrased: You

have sat here too long for any good you have done here. In the name of God, go!

Morning In American? No. But Merry Christmas Will Do Just Fine

On the eve of Christmas 2015, to distinguish from years past, everybody this writer encountered, informally, appeared unafraid to loudly wish me a "Merry Christmas." Is it a mere coincidence that, for once, more Americans are proclaiming their Christian customs as openly as they are hankering for less Islam and immigration? These are very modest things, if you think about it. I am hardly here making for the Trump presidential candidacy the messianic claims Obama made for his term. At his nomination victory speech, circa 2008, in St. Paul, Minnesota, Obama was hubris and hyperbole rolled in one. Remember his, "This was the moment when the rise of the oceans began to slow and our planet began to heal" flight of fancy?

Vaporized Obama:

> [T]his was the moment when we ended a war and secured our nation and restored our image as the last, best hope on Earth. This was the moment—this was the time—when we came together to remake this great nation so that it may always reflect our very best selves, and our highest ideals.

So, was the Obama presidency good for you? Did the earth move? Only if, in the words of southern statesman John C. Calhoun, you belong to a portion of the community that "receives in disbursements more than it pays in taxes," starting with oink-sector employees.

Or, if you take delight in being dressed down daily for the existential sin of "whiteness."

In any event, if Donald Trump has heralded the first politically incorrect Christmas in years, this Jew thinks it's dandy.

No Political Criminal Record

When Mr. Trump began exploring his political prospects, in earnest, Congressman Ron Paul tossed and gored the businessman and so did this libertarian. I'm not proud of having used "megalomaniacal" to describe Mr. Trump, in January of 2011. Still, a column, "Sinophobia Trumps Common Sense," made points still valid:

> The business mogul is motivated by the sense that the nimbus of great power that surrounds the U.S. is dissipating. It hasn't occurred to him to search closer to home for the causes of America's economic anemia—at Fanny, Freddie, and the Fed, for a start. Since Trump has no idea what's potting, and is not eager to look in his own plate—he blames OPEC and

China for the burdens of doing business in the U.S.

As early as 2011, I cynically denounced, "the Trump plan to reclaim global greatness and glory," which "included a strategy America has yet to try: the use of force, of course."

Strutting around on the world stage, showing those Saudis and Chinese who's boss: This may serve as a perfect panacea for the deficiencies in Trump's persona, but is hardly a solution to U.S. woes, at home or abroad. Sadly, Sinophobia is sanctioned among American opinion makers. The dislike for China falls within the realm of perfectly respectable economic theory. Accordingly, the Chinese have levered themselves out of poverty not through industry, frugality and ambition, but by manipulating their money and stealing American intellectual property.

That was then—and although nowhere has this libertarian declared in support of Donald Trump (or changed her view on Sinophobia), it has been my intention to advance an analysis of The Positive Process that is Trump. *A close reading of The Trump Revolution will reveal that matters of process are being underscored, such as the differences between political incentives in operation and apolitical incentives in operation: Trump's.*

Trump cannot be compared, on the meta-level, to a politician. What do I mean?

When Trump filed his financial disclosure with the Federal Election Commission, in July of 2015, the bobbing heads of CNN snickered and smirked first and then resorted to impugning his motives. In declaring for president, asserted our never-humble TV hosts, Trump was merely "boasting" of his upwards of ten billion worth. (What's there to be humble about?) Trump was running to "glorify" Trump. Unable to come to terms with Trump's grassroots-supported ascent, media cretins had taken to comforting themselves with a flight from reality and reason. Predicted a prototype press person at *National Journal*: "Name ID and support from the GOP base may be boosting Trump for now, but it will fade." Echoed the rest at The Trump-In-Decline School Of Alternate Reality: "Trump's just building a brand"—this as the Trump business brand suffered the brunt of his positions in boycotts as far as Dubai.

While his political rivals are sponsored by super PAC puppet masters, *Trump is putting-up and pledging to the American People a chunk of his life, his fortune and sacred honor.* Why is he, then, asked to prove the nobility of his motivates, and not his adversaries, who're, essentially, nothing but kept, political courtesans? Besides, to infer motivation—to allege self-aggrandizement here—amounts to psychologizing. And to psychologize is to make a logically invalid argument. Psychologizing, it can be argued, is an extension of the *ad hominem* argument: The habit of insulting and impugning an opponent's character, rather than addressing the logic or illogic of his positions and actions. To mouth about "motivation" is logically invalid because the motivation behind an individual's deeds can seldom be divined.

We can reliably judge an actor only by his actions.

Still, we know a good deal about the "motivation" of Trump's rivals, members of the political class. Over them, Donald Trump has a profound and substantial moral lead. He's no career politician, like the rest of his rivals, bar Ben Carson. All live off the American people, parasitically, and have grown wealthy through the coercive use of state power. Consider: If you despise Mr. Rubio, and wish to withdraw tax dimes from contributing to Rubio's bloated salary, the engorged wages of his staff, office expenses, taxpayer supported book promotions and tours, travel; retirement, life insurance, Cadillac healthcare plan, paid vacations and other subsidies and perks in perpetuity—you can't! Compelled you are to provide for this neoconservative and for all other political parasites in office. On the other hand, Mr. Trump has never forced me or you to frequent his resorts or pay for his personal choices and life style. In the tradition of America's Founders, Trump has, moreover, already foresworn compensation should he be elected president of the United States. Had Bush, Cruz, Rubio and the rest been prepared to serve *sans* salary, you'd never hear the end of it; they'd have emblazoned the skies with slogans:

"Working for you, working for free."

Other than his position statements, *Trump has no policy making past. In the nomenclature of law, Trump's record is clean.* The candidate has no political criminal record. (Come to think of it, El Chapo has a cleaner criminal record than the last two American presidents: He had fewer people killed.)

Corruption Codified In Law

To appreciate the importance of Trump's financial independence—and, by logical extension, his moral superiority over his rivals—it's essential to grasp how corrupt to the core Washington is and, consequently, the significance of his standing apart of it and being independent of it. The corruption, moreover, is codified in law. "Revolving door lobbyists" is a term in political science that denotes the seamless passing of legislators, administration officials and congressional staffers from their seats in the halls of power to "lucrative jobs representing the very industries they regulate." This rot is not outlawed and prosecuted, but regulated just sufficiently to throw inquisitive minds off scent. (See "Revolving door lobbyists and interest representation," by Timothy M LaPiraa and Herschel F Thomas, in *Interest Groups & Advocacy*, 2014.)

Are We Rome? by Cullen Murphy further draws the unflattering parallels between the imperial rule of ancient Rome and that of modern America, down to the contemporary musicians (like patrons of Obama's court Beyoncé and Jay-Z), "the courtesans, diviners, buffoons [categories are not mutually exclusive] ... the people who taste the emperor's food before he himself does ... the core groups of bureaucrats and toadies who function within the nimbus of great power."

The domain name "USA.gov," if you will.

Lest you forget, the D.C. hood is also home to your favorite, oh-so gritty media personalities, who gather inside or near the Bubble to reap "the benefits of being at the center of the Imperium." Prior to the Iowa Caucuses, one such honest insider, commentator Tucker Carlson, finally came clean—also code for rocking the ship of state just enough to retain street cred with "the folks":

> ... let's pretend for a second this isn't Washington. Let's imagine it's the capital of an African country, say Burkina Faso, and we are doing a study on corruption. Probably the first question we'd ask: How many government officials have close relatives who make a living by influencing government spending? A huge percentage of them? OK. Case closed. Ouagadougou is obviously a very corrupt city. That's how the rest of the country views D.C. Washington is probably the richest city in America because the people who live there have the closest proximity to power. That seems obvious to most voters. It's less obvious to us, because everyone here is so cheerful and familiar, and we're too close to it. Chairman so-

and-so's son-in-law lobbies the committee? That
doesn't seem corrupt. He's such a good guy.

A remarkable documentary televised by Sean Hannity of
the Fox News Channel, in 2013, saw "Peter Schweizer, the
president and co-founder of the Government Accountability
Institute, and Stephen K. Bannon, the executive chairman of
Breitbart News and co-founder of the Government
Accountability Institute," join to "investigate what they call
crony capitalism among the city's power elite and the tactics
used by lobbyists, bureaucrats and legislators to finance their
lifestyles with taxpayer money," to quote Wynton Hall of
Breitbart.com.

When it comes to their dispensation *vis-a-vis* the people,
the Republican and Democratic parties are "two wings of
the same bird of prey," in the words of another wag.
There's not a dime's worth of difference between the
parties when it comes to the ultimate goal of members as
judged by their deeds:

> "The wealth," explained Schweizer, "comes from
> extracting it from the rest of the country. Boom
> town is something that no one in Washington
> wants to talk about. When they do, they tend to
> blame the other side. But the reality is today that
> in Washington, D.C., the business is ... money.
> ... There is a business model there. And really
> what exists is what we call the permanent
> political class. We think of Republicans and

Democrats and there are philosophical differences. At the end of the day, they are all primarily looking for ways to make money. And you don't make money by shrinking government. You make money by growing government. ... that's why nothing changes in Washington, that's why you have these budget debates. And like you said, you're talking about cuts in growth rates of budgets, not cut in the budgets."

In Washington, where the "per capita income is now higher than Silicon Valley," wealth is *extracted*, not *created*.

The local Native Americans named the river Potomac which means where goods are offloaded or where tribute is paid. Today that tribute comes in the form of trillions of dollars of taxpayer money that flood into this city every year. ... America's previous boom towns became wealthy because they produced something. ... *It's not that money controls Washington. Washington controls the money.* It's a business model. [There's] an industrial logic to this business model [and it is] to extract power from the rest of the country in money [and move it] into [the] centralized location which is Washington. ... *That business model is government.* And it's bigger government. And as long as you have the ability to borrow ... As long as they can take tax receipts and borrow, they're going to continue to do that. ("Welcome to BoomTown: Washington, D.C.," Fox News, January 25, 2013. Italics added.)

Ultimately, "All life in Washington today derives ... from the capital's own version of Rome's annona—the continuous infusion not of grain and olive oil but of tax revenue and borrowed money," writes Murphy. "Instead of ships and barges there are banks, 10,000 of them designated for this purpose, which funnel the nation's tax payments to the city. This 'never-ending flow of revenue creates a broad level of affluence that has no real counterpart anywhere in America. Washington simply doesn't look like the rest of America." But its residents "fail to view this as bizarre."

Thanks to the graft flowing into the Beltway, the average income in and around Washington D.C. is $85,189 compared to $49,777 for the hinterland, where unemployment rates are almost double. For their part, the people of the provinces have been programmed to go on pilgrimages to D.C., and genuflect to their opulent oppressors. The rest exist merely to serve the masters of modern Rome.

As Chapter 4 of this volume explains, "A fish rots from the head down." To do business, the country's capitalists are forced to court politicians, a reality brought about by corrupt politics:

> A successful politician and a successful businessman represent two solitudes, never the twain shall meet—except when the capitalist must curry favor with the politician so as to further his business interests ... Trump's donations to both parties fit a pattern forced by the regulatory state, whereby, in order to keep doing business; business is compelled to buy-off politicians.

Until now, the rest of the country hasn't much flinched about the fleecing. Yes, we had the Tea Party and the Occupy Wall Street movements. Ultimately, voters still filed into the booths and voted establishment. No more. *The electorate is demanding a representative differently incentivized than the career politician.*

Trump doesn't need the lucrative, predatory and coercive political process to increase his riches; the obverse is true. The man's thinking and methods are utterly at odds with politics. As he put it plainly, "I'm owned by the people!" Not by MSM (mainstream media), not by super PACS (political action committees), not by lobbyists—Arabs or Jews—not even by AIPAC, the American Israel Public Affairs Committee, whose bidding most Republicans obediently do. In fact, Trump was subjected to loud booing when he told a Jewish-Republican crowd he couldn't be bought. If anything, Trump's promise to be a "neutral guy" in attempting to broker an Israel-Palestinian peace agreement has given "hawkish candidates room to pounce."

By an amazing coincidence, so did Ted Cruz. For someone who's supposed to be so smart, Cruz has made some asinine arguments. By claiming Trump is part of the D.C. corruption because (like all business moguls), Trump has effectively paid politicians to let him operate—career politician Cruz is blaming the victim of government predation. Not all corruption is created equal. Take away government, and there would be no such unseemly collusion. For government has a monopoly over the use of force in society; entrepreneurs have no police power behind them. If business fails to pacify government, the businessman will go under or be perp-walked to prison. A crony capitalist is still in a bondage relationship, where his Securities and Exchange dominator is the one cracking the whip.

The Scarlet Letter 'E'

In this magnificent upheaval underway in American party politics, fans of the Fox News Channel should take a moment to consider why it is that most of the network's anchors and bobbing heads, neoconservatives in particular, have been as livid as liberals over the ongoing revolt in the Republican base. The reason is that FNC is mainstream media. In its approach to Donald Trump, Fox News even set the rancorous tone to the presidential debates, with a performance almost as odious as that of the openly leftist CNBC.

At any rate, Trump has rendered the insider honorific a liability at FNC. A show, "Political Insiders," may be forced to change its name now that the term has become a pejorative. Indeed, a November 1, 2015 segment saw regular Doug Schoen renounce his insider label. Then and there did pollster Schoen declare himself an outsider. The former "long-time Clinton insider" may no longer be in with the Clintons, but he is the consummate insider in Republican circles; a Democrat domesticated by Republican insiders.

The cable commentariat is a cog in the corpulent D.C. fleshpot. Quipped *New York Magazine* media writer Gabriel Sherman (as relayed by Newsmax.com): "[T]the GOP presidential front-runner has loosened 'the grip that [Fox News owner] Rupert Murdoch [network boss], Roger Ailes, and Co. have held on the GOP for nearly a generation."

Yes, the rats are abandoning the sinking ship-of-state. Mr. Trump has begun a process. It's a positive process in as much as it threatens to shatter an ossified, corrupt, intertwined political system. *The endorsement forthcoming in this space, to repeat, is of this process, the outcome of which might see a single individual weaken the chains that bind each one of us to an oppressive, centralized authority and to the system that serves and sustains it.*

In chronicling and analyzing the genesis of the Trump surge, starting in June of 2015, a composite has emerged. The collection that is *The Trump Revolution* reveals a man, not a mouse, as Bernie Sanders most assuredly is.

Refreshingly, The Political Trump is no different to Citizen Trump. What you see is what you get.

Unlike America's northeastern elites and their brethren in Britain and Brussels, Mr. Trump, moreover, is genuinely fond of the Common American.

A Love For The People

Donald Trump is unlikely to be caught off-guard mouthing his contempt for small-town America, as Barack Obama did in depicting potential voters as clinging to their guns, god and other bigotries. It's hard to imagine Mr. Trump ever demonstrating the cruelty and hypocrisy of a Gordon Brown, Great Britain's former prime minister. In May of 2010, after hearing Mrs. Gillian Duffy's worries over deficits and immigration, the pompous, two-faced boor of a prime minister retreated to his limousine, and, microphone on, proceeded to berate this perfectly decent lady, calling her "horrible," "old woman," and "bigoted."

The Trump revolution is the last heave-ho of America's Mrs. Duffys; of America's historic, founding majority.

Likewise have Republicans and Democrats maligned Trump's Middle America as worthy of contempt. "Undereducated," hissed prissy schoolmarm Kathleen Parker, a writer who's been amply rewarded in the U.S. for having never written anything remotely original, edgy or interesting. (A Christopher Hitchens witticism is apposite here. It encapsulates the banal, epistolary enterprise of the Kathleen Parker Republicans and the Joan Walsh

Democrats: "What is original is not true and what is true is not original.") Nothing but "downscale whites," derided Democratic strategist Steve McMahon, on *Hardball*, in early January.

The Trump Revolution collection inadvertently showcases a man who won't grovel to The Powers That Be and who has refused to submit to the precepts of cultural Marxism, namely the tyranny that sees speech policed for impropriety and individuals stigmatized and isolated for thinking and speaking in a manner disallowed by the politically correct police. Whatever transpires in the election year ahead, the Trump revolution is the revolt mainstream media missed and, when it finally cottoned-on to what was unfolding, continued to wish away every day.

The Trump Revolution takes the reader through Trump's political progression in real time, when the essays featured were penned, from the time Mr. Trump was polling at twelve percent and trailing the "low energy" Jeb Bush, to Trump's triumphant forty-one percent plus popularity, through his somewhat disappointing showing in Iowa and triumphs in New Hampshire, South Carolina and Nevada; to his sweeping successes on Super Tuesday I (March 1), Super Saturday (March 5), the winner-take-all super-duper Tuesday (March 15), the vanquishing of his rivals in New York State (April 19), a week later in Maryland, Pennsylvania, Connecticut, Delaware and Rhode Island. And in Indiana. After that five-for-five victory on April 26, someone had to finally say it:

"I consider myself the presumptive nominee."

Opening Statement: Welcome To The Post-Constitutional Jungle

After Indiana, it was game, set, match. And when the magic number of delegates was obtained, "1237" became the new "300" (a reference to the comic-book rendition of the epic Battle of Thermopylae in 480 BC).

Essays have been fleshed out for the reader's edification. Their impetus, however, remains unchanged. Their predictive power obtains. This is more than one can say about the columnar output of, say, Chucky Krauthammer, neoconservative prize fighter in the Fox News corner. Chucky, who had called Trump a "rodeo clown," last summer—and has only just begun to correct course—might as well chuck everything he's written about Trump's meteoric ascent, because the material's predictive, analytical value is ... zero. Krauthammer is in the majority.

While *The Trump Revolution* deconstructs the evolution of the Political Trump, this book, at the same time, applauds The Donald's creative destruction. A masculine force at full tilt, Mr. Trump has been creating a new reality on the ground. This political Samson is bringing a den of iniquity, crashing down around him.

1. A CANDIDATE TO 'KICK THE CRAP OUT OF ALL THE POLITICIANS'

Since he announced for president, real-estate tycoon Donald Trump has distinguished himself from the pack of Republican presidential hopefuls. Trump claims he opposed the invasion of Iraq. If this is true, it would make him better than almost all his Republican competitors, who mulishly continue to justify the most disastrous military campaign in American history (besides the War Between The States).

Decisive and to the point was Trump about liberalizing ties with Cuba: "It's time!" he stated. The man who wrote *The Art of The Deal*, however, would rather a "deal" with Cuba favored ordinary Americans and Cubans, and would know how to "deliver the goods."

We inhabit a world of managed, not free, trade. Trump is no rent-seeking political rat like every other Republican competing for the throne (besides Ben Carson, who is similarly motivated). Better than any self-interested politician, Trump can probably negotiate winning deals on all Treaties in Force, to the benefit of Americans.

"I'm really rich," Trump swanked disarmingly. Being independently and stupendously wealthy means that this American individualist can continue to march to his own drumbeat; be as blunt and bold as he wants and pander to nobody. His "fellow GOP presidential candidates," explained Trump, are "totally controlled by their donors, by the lobbyists and by the special interests. If we have another politician, this country's going down. ... I've watched the politicians; I've dealt with them all my life. They will never make America great again. They don't even have a chance."

In the productive, non-parasitical economy, Trump has been enormously successful. Career politicians have created the hot mess that is America. The Founding Fathers wanted regular citizens to serve the public, not live off it as a vocation. Such upstanding Americans were to return to their careers after serving.

The consummate *homo economicus*, Trump is a rational actor in the market place. Unlike the rest of the GOP contenders who're guided by political calculations; Trump speaks like a man to whom rational economic choices are second nature. And so he gets that the "stock market is bloated"; that the Stock Exchange is a laughing stock, and that soaring stock prices are a consequence of centrally planned, monetary stimulus.

The business mogul surprised Fox News' Bill O'Reilly with the revelation that he'd "have a great relationship with Vladimir Putin." This is a good thing. Whereas in the past, Trump was motivated by the sense that "the nimbus of great power that surrounds the U.S. was dissipating"—he now seems prepared to search closer to home for the causes of America's economic inertia.

Also to O'Reilly, Trump "promised to build a wall along the southern border and make Mexico pay for it. "The

Factor" host stated that there's no way they will pay for it."
Although Bill is likelier than Dana Perino to comprehend
the workings of tax and trade policy, Trump opted to calm
the host down: "You have to let me handle that. They will
pay for the wall, and the wall will go up." D.C. insider
Perino hit the roof: "On what planet is that actually true?
Do you think you can make Mexico pay for a permanent
wall between Mexico and the United States?" You can do
that?"

A guide to the perpetually perplexed: Trump must be
thinking of taking the populist path advocated by Patrick J.
Buchanan, whose patriotism is unimpeachable: tariffs.
Levying a tariff on Mexico could indeed pay for a wall. *Trade
tariffs are not this libertarian's bag. But walling off the deluge of
Democrats crossing the southwest border is.*

Finally, Trump is annoying the right people—from the
liberal media to regimist neoconservatives like Perino and
Charles Krauthammer, to noise-making musician and
socialist Neil Young. In particular is the MSM furious about
Trump's matter-of-fact, informed assertion as to the quality
of America's largest immigrant population.

Donald Trump: "When Mexico sends its people,
they're not sending their best. They're not sending you. ...
They're sending people that have lots of problems and
they're bringing those problems with [them]. They're
bringing drugs. They're bringing crime. They're rapists.
And some, I assume, are good people. But I speak to border
guards, and they tell us what they're getting."

Brooke Baldwin, CNN: "... The notion of calling Mexicans rapists, people lose their jobs over words like those. And this is a man running for the president of the United States."

Barbie, Trump created his job. He owns it.

And The Donald has certainly apprised himself of the facts. Perhaps he is reading Ann Coulter's data-driven *Adios America!* in which she writes: "The U.S. government admits that at least 351,000 criminal immigrants were incarcerated [by] the United States as of 2011—the vast majority of them Mexican." (*Report to Congressional Requesters*, 7 and 10.)

By the General Accountability Office's "extremely conservative figures, Mexicans alone—forget other immigrants—have murdered a minimum of 23,000 Americans in the last few decades," as compared to the Jihadis' 4000 for the same time-frame.

I know, stick to rape; murder doesn't matter. Cited in *Adios* is a report from the Inter-American Children's Institute. It seconds what the media-political-complex has submerged. "Latin America is second only to Asia in the sexual exploitation of women and children because sex abuse is 'ingrained [in] the minds of the people.' Women and children are 'seen as objects instead of human beings with rights and freedoms.'" (p. 168)

Ann's *Adios* provides a critical-mass of evidence for Trumps impolitic statement. A few of Latin America's proud sons are:

• Ariel Castro (kidnapper, sexual sadist, operated out of Cleveland)
• Elias Acevedo (173 counts of rape, 115 of kidnapping, Castro's neighbor)
• Ingmar Cuandique (killer of Chandra Levy)
• Matias Reyes (contributor, Central Park rape)
• Conrado Juarez and family accomplices (Baby Hope's rape and murder)

Adios cites well-concealed official records to uncover a preponderance of "Hispanic child rapists," rounded up (and often released again), in "Nebraska, Indiana, even Hawaii." When rates of child pregnancies and births are factored-in as proxies for rape; Latin America's rape culture on American soil becomes even scarier.

Trump is on to something elusive: the truth. RedState's Erick Erickson concurs (kind of). "Trump's campaign," he writes," "makes a hell of a lot of sense in an age when people no longer think their vote matters, but they sure want the crap kicked out of all the politicians they blame for making their vote meaningless."

Get cracking, Donald.

~ June 19, 2015

2. NO TRUMP APOLOGY TOUR

CNN anchor Don Lemon conducted an interview with Donald Trump. It went very well, for Mr. Trump, that is. So well that Lemon's scoop was difficult to locate on CNN's website. Instead, Mediate.com scooped the telephonic exchange.

Lemon was at a loss. He got more sour-looking by the minute, as Trump bulldozed him with the force of his convictions and personality. There was no interrupting Trump's train of thought. The "builder-businessman" was going to say his piece. And Americans have been listening intently.

"A CNN/ORC poll released Wednesday," reported *National Journal*, "showed Trump had twelve percent of the vote among Republicans and Republican-leaners, second only to former Florida Gov. Jeb Bush, who earned nineteen percent." Trump's retort: "I'm not happy being behind Jeb Bush." He went on to ponder how Bush III (a man he would fire) could be soaring in the polls:

> I don't get it. He's in favor of Common Core, extremely weak on immigration. He thinks people come over for love. I don't understand why he's in first place. Maybe it's the Bush name. Last thing we need is another Bush. But I will tell you, I'm a little surprised he's in the position he's in.

As Trump sees it, his countrymen are being betrayed by The Beltway. To make America great, he'd have to restore American prosperity. Jeb Bush will not do America's bidding. It's not his thing. Jeb Bush will not lead America to the Promised Land, in Trump's words. No politician will. The hope is that Trump, who does not need to ride us like the others, will get the parasites-in waiting off our backs.

Trump's strength is that he keeps coming back to the stuff of life: business, economics, making a living. Politics is the stuff that kills all that.

To Trump, actions are measured by their outcomes. Mitt Romney, by Romney's own admission, "left everything on the field." He gave his all in the 2012 presidential campaign. But from Trump's perspective, "Romney did a poor job." He didn't win. "It's a race that should have been won," Trump insisted.

Still, Lemon kept trying to trip Trump: "You're being clobbered by Republican leaderships." While voters take Donald Trump very seriously; his party's leadership does not.

But Trump knew better. He was not going to keep the GOP's dirty little secrets. He doesn't have to; he can fund his own political action committee. Yes, his rivals, opponents, the consultants, Rudy Giuliani—they may go on TV to denounce him; make light of him. But his lead in the polls is making that harder. Behind the scenes, the schemers are calling on Trump, sending him little love notes.

Lemon fastened his limp-wristed grip. Trump's ostensible lack of gravitas was the tack to take: "Will you really be there on the stage with the other Republican candidates?" the anchor persisted in disbelief. A pumped Trump snapped, "Why would I not?!" He, Trump, had attended the Wharton School of Business; was a great student at one of the toughest schools to get into; went on to make a tremendous fortune; wrote a business book that became the bestselling business book of all time; built a great company, employed tens of thousands of people over the years, and is a great success. How is he, Trump, unfit to stand on stage with "some governor who is nothing, and some senator who is not very good and has not done a good job?!" Note that Trump resorts to self-praise, primarily, when denigrated by denizens of the political process. People have forgotten. So he must remind them: Success is about creating value for people in the free market; not wielding force against them in the political arena.

Our country is being run by people who don't know what they're doing. Our politicians are not smart. I want our country to thrive. And: Illegal immigration is killing our country. You got to have a border. If you don't have a border, you don't have a country.

Lemon was aghast. Truth has that effect on the gormless. The anchor shifted the focus to Macy's fit of pique, hoping he'd score some points against Trump in that department. The department store had discontinued Trump's clothing line. Donald was "divisive," Macy's whined.

Trump's one-two punch: "Macy's folded under pressure. It's not a big business for me; it's very small. It's ties and stuff. It's a peanut. CEO Terry Lundgren folded under pressure. That's the problem with our country; everyone folds under pressure. Two picketers arrive outside Macy's and the store folds. People can't handle pressure. *That's OK with me*. It's a very small business; *let them do what they want to do*. You have to ride through the pressure. They can't handle pressure. It's fine."

Would that militant gay couples were as tolerant toward the poor baker who doesn't want to bake them a wedding cake as Trump is toward those who shun his business.

The unremitting influx of peasants pouring over the U.S. border with Mexico is having a disastrous impact on America—on crime rates, urban sprawl, traffic congestion, overcrowding, pollution, infrastructure, the loss of rural and protected land and species. Malfunctioning media—overbearing fools like Fox News' ubiquitous Juan Williams—believe Trump's pronouncements on these effects is "divisive."

Au contraire. Trump's impolitic truth-telling seems to have *united* a hell of a lot of hopeless Americans.

The best of Trump Lemon left for last. "Is there anything you'd like to clear up while I have you here?"

"Nothing, absolutely nothing," Donald fired back.

There will be no Trump apology tour.

~ July 3, 2015

3. DOES MCCAIN OWE MEA CULPA TO POWS AND MEN MISSING IN ACTION?

"It's the beginning of the end for Donald Trump." "It disqualifies him as a presidential candidate." "This is the end of his run." So crowed the political operatives looking to take down Mr. Trump, and by so doing, protect the political *status quo* and ease themselves into positions of greater power. The egos in the anchor's chair and the pundits opposite chimed in: "He'll make the more serious candidates look more serious," predicted the next Michael Oakeshott, Republican pundit S. E. Cupp.

The Donald is in the dock for desecrating one of the political establishment's most sacred cows: Arizona Senator John McCain. Speaking at a forum in Iowa, the popular presidential hopeful said these sagacious things about the Republican from Arizona: "[McCain's] not a war hero. He is a war hero because he was captured. I like people that weren't captured, okay?" (On the same occasion, Trump ventured that he was not particularly for the Vietnam War, a position that should endear him to principled libertarians.)

Not only does Donald Trump not owe Senator McCain an apology; McCain likely owes *mea culpa* to Trump—and to the very many Vietnam veterans and their families whom he is alleged to have betrayed. Yes, the heroic prisoner-of-war pedigree upon which McCain has established his career and credibility is probably a myth.

For our purposes, the story begins with Sydney Schanberg, back in the days before American journalism became a circle jerk of power brokers. Mr. Schanberg is one of "America's most eminent journalists." "For his accounts of the fall of Cambodia to the Khmer Rouge in 1975," Schanberg "was awarded the Pulitzer Prize for international reporting 'at great risk.' He is also the recipient of many other awards—including two George Polk awards, two Overseas Press Club awards and the Sigma Delta Chi prize for distinguished journalism." Schanberg's byline at *The Nation* magazine further reveals that:

> The 1984 movie, 'The Killing Fields,' which won several Academy Awards, was based on his book *The Death and Life of Dith Pran*—a memoir of his experiences covering the war in Cambodia for the New York Times and of his relationship with his Cambodian colleague, Dith Pran.

Schanberg is also the author of a "remarkable 8,000-word exposé": "McCain and the POW Cover-Up." Here follow the opening paragraphs, courtesy of The Unz Review. They provide a *précis* of the forensic evidence collected against McCain by Schanberg, ally of Vietnam War prisoners of war (POW) and men missing in action (MIA):

John McCain, who has risen to political prominence on his image as a Vietnam POW war hero, has, inexplicably, worked very hard to hide from the public stunning information about American prisoners in Vietnam who, unlike him, didn't return home. Throughout his Senate career, McCain has quietly sponsored and pushed into federal law a set of prohibitions that keep the most revealing information about these men buried as classified documents. Thus, the war hero people would logically imagine to be a determined crusader for the interests of POWs and their families; became instead the strange champion of hiding the evidence and closing the books. ...

... The sum of the secrets McCain has sought to hide is not small. There exists a telling mass of official documents, radio intercepts, witness depositions, satellite photos of rescue symbols that pilots were trained to use, electronic messages from the ground containing the individual code numbers given to airmen, a rescue mission by a Special Forces unit that was aborted twice by Washington and even sworn testimony by two defense secretaries that 'men were left behind.' This imposing body of evidence suggests that a large number—probably hundreds—of the US prisoners held in Vietnam were not returned when the peace treaty was signed in January 1973 and Hanoi released 591 men, among them Navy combat pilot John S. McCain.

The Pentagon had been withholding significant information from POW families for years. What's more, the Pentagon's POW/MIA operation had been publicly shamed by internal whistleblowers and POW families for holding back documents as part of a policy of 'debunking' POW intelligence even when the information was obviously credible. The pressure from the families and Vietnam veterans finally produced the creation, in late 1991, of a Senate 'Select Committee on POW/MIA Affairs.' The chair was John Kerry, but McCain, as a POW, was its most pivotal member. In the end, the committee became part of the debunking machine. ...

A tale that has more twists than a serpent's tail would be incomplete without mentioning another newsman, Ron Unz. First in his capacity as publisher of *The American Conservative* (July 1, 2010 cover story), and currently as editor-in-chief of The Unz Review—Mr. Unz has kept Schanberg's voluminously sourced and criminally underexposed exposé alive in the alternative (intelligent) media.

Schanberg's own journalistic and military man's instincts were first piqued when 'military officers [he] knew from that conflict began coming to [him] with maps and POW sightings and depositions by Vietnamese witnesses.' Having served 'in the Army in Germany during the Cold War and witnessing combat firsthand as a reporter in India and Indochina,' Schanberg had 'great respect for those who fight for their country.' To my mind,' he explained, 'we dishonored U.S. troops when our government failed to bring them home from Vietnam after the 591 others were released—and then claimed they didn't exist. And politicians dishonor themselves when they pay lip service to the bravery and sacrifice of soldiers only to leave untold numbers behind, rationalizing to themselves that it's merely one of the unfortunate costs of war.'

The man is clearly not an intemperate sort. Some would say that to knowingly leave servicemen behind in the service of political ambition is treason.

Despite his position "as one of the highest-ranking editors at the *New York Times*," Schanberg was forced to unmask Hanoi John, on September 18, 2008, in *The Nation* magazine. He recounts: "I took the data to the appropriate desks [at the *New York Times*] and suggested it was material worth pursuing. There were no takers."

In the war-hero department, McCain is manifestly more beloved by the *bien pensant* elites than his "Democratic counterpart," Vietnam Medal of Honor recipient Democrat Bob Kerrey. While not a "single mention of McCain's role in burying information about POWs" is to be found in the annals of the *New York Times*; the paper of record—"a compliment [rightly] used these days as a cudgel"—took upon itself to expose Bob Kerrey (in its magazine) for having "ordered his men to massacre over a dozen innocent Vietnamese civilians—women, children, and infants," in February of 1969.

McMussolini's more recent record of devastation is an organic extension of his mythologized past: "John McCain the politician," wrote Trump in a *USA Today* editorial, "has made America less safe, sent our brave soldiers into wrong-headed foreign adventures, covered up for President Obama with the VA scandal and has spent most of his time in the Senate pushing amnesty. He would rather protect the Iraqi border than Arizona's."

Were Donald to dig deeper, he'd discover that McCain as champion of prisoners-of-war and men missing-in-action is as dubious as "John McCain the politician."

~July 24, 2015

4. TRUMP SHOULD TRIANGULATE

Working people warm to Donald Trump. He appeals to a good segment of real Americans. The American media, however, lacks the depth and understanding to grasp the fellow-feeling Trump engenders in his fans.

Political Power Vs. Economic Power

To understand why his campaign has legs, it is necessary to grasp the difference between The Donald and The Career Politician. Why so? Because although his supporters can ill-articulate these differences, they live them and feel them viscerally. Their reaction to Mr. Trump is informed by a sense of Trump the private citizen, the businessman, the anti-politician. As such, they grasp that Trump's reality, incentives and motives sharply diverge from those of the professional politician. His reasons for doing what he's doing are different.

Differently put: A successful politician and a successful businessman represent two solitudes, never the twain shall meet—except when the capitalist must curry favor with the politician so as to further his business interests, a reality brought about by corrupt politics. Trump's donations to both parties fit a pattern forced by the Regulatory State, whereby, in order to keep doing business; business is compelled to buy-off politicians.

"What, then, is the difference between economic power and political power?"

Capitalism.org supplies a succinct reply:

"The difference between political and economic power is the difference between plunder and production, between punishment and reward, between destruction and trade. Plunder, punishment, and destruction belong to the political realm; production, reward, and trade belong to the economic realm."

By definition, a professional politician is opportunistic and parasitic. For his survival, he must feed off his hosts. To convince the host to let him hook on and drain his lifeblood, the political hookworm must persuade enough of them to believe his deception. The energies of this political confidence trickster are thus focused on gaining voter confidence by promising what will *never* be delivered and what is *impossible* to deliver.

The methods of politics, encapsulated in the title of broadcaster Mark Levin's latest book, are deceit and plunder, in that order. (And no, Mr. Levin, electing a conservative will not transform this *modus operandi*.) The machinery of politics is coercion and force. If elected, a politician gains power over those who did not support him as well as over those who supported him. Once in power, and backed by police power, he revels in the right to legislate and regulate vast areas in the lives of people.

Conversely, to succeed, a man in the private economy must deliver on his promises. If he doesn't fulfill his promises, he loses his shirt. He goes belly up.

Whereas success in politics depends on intellectual deceit and economic plunder; success in the private economy indicates that an individual has delivered on his promises: he has provided goods and services people want, built buildings and resorts they inhabit and frequent, provided his investors with a return on their investment. And he has done so using the peaceful, voluntary means of free-market capitalism. He has not passed an individual mandate to compel any and all to patronize his buildings, businesses or buy his products.

Flawed though he most certainly is—Donald Trump belongs to the category of Americans who wield economic power.

Trump has had moral and business failings aplenty. He has taken risks for which he has paid with his capital and good name. (He certainly owes recompense to the Scottish farmers of Aberdeenshire, whose lives he upended with his golf resort development, in 2011.) Not given to the contemplative life, Trump is a pragmatist. He has waded into some very polluted waters. But he swims. He doesn't drown.

To that people relate.

Raping Reality With Political Theory

For his credibility, the politician cloaks himself in the raiment of political theory, cobbled up by liberal academics. Theory that controverts reality is his stock-in-trade. And so the politician, Democrat and Republican, will conjure "ideas"—delusional ideation really—that flout reason, the nature of man, and the natural laws of justice and economics.

People, however, are smart. They sense the discrepancy between contrived political theory and reality; between conceptual frameworks that do not reflect reality, but rape it.

Examples: The macroeconomics parroted by Democrats and Republicans dictate that economic recessions and depressions must be cured by increasing the availability of easy credit so that more spending can take place. People know this is bogus. They know they cannot "deficit" spend themselves into prosperity. Why, then, would the "country" manage to disregard the immutable laws of economics?

From the safety and comfort of rarefied zip codes, open-border theorists tutor the little people in the positive economic effects on productivity and economic growth of, say, high population density. But regular folks don't have to travel to Cairo or Karachi to discover that this urban theory is an urban myth.

The same sort of thing happens in the hearts and minds of ordinary working men and women when Trump says Crimea is Europe's problem (and, subsequently, that "North Korea is China's problem to fix"). Yes, let regional powers like Germany and China police their neighborhoods.

Or, when Trump reveals that he pays as little tax as he can. "I hate what our country does with our taxes." A noble sentiment, because true.

In her Daily Bell column, libertarian theorist Wendy McElroy explains why certain verities are second-nature: "The more basic the political issue or principle, the more likely it is to be understood by most people and to appeal to their interests." For example, despite pronouncements from up high that "the common man should not be allowed to judge the law" because he lacks intellectual sophistication, "the trial by jury lauded by Lysander Spooner was meant to place community opinion as a safeguard between the individual and the State. As Spooner explained, 'The trial by jury is a trial by the country—that is, by the people—as distinguished from a trial by the government ... The object ... is to guard against every species of oppression by the government.'"

Party Pooper

That Trump is no "GOP loyalist" hardly disqualifies him from representing the Republican base, which the GOP habitually misrepresents. Given the GOP's record; a failure to swear fealty to the Republican Party is an award-worthy failing.

On the topic of awards, James Webb, the decorated Marine who served as Ronald Reagan's secretary of the navy, is no GOP loyalist, either. Webb, indisputably the last salt-of-the-earth Democrat, had considered a bid for president as a Democrat, appearing at the first Clinton-dominated debate in October of 2015.

Trump would do well to triangulate, *à la* Bill Clinton, and place the talented Mr. Webb on the Trump ticket. Then, make immigration a central theme in the campaign, advance a principled, major, pro-black policy by speaking to the legalization or decriminalizing of drug use and sale—and Trump will have secured the vote of blacks, white southern Democrats and other Reagan Democrats. Like no other, drug legalization is a proxy black issue, worthy of the endorsement of the "Black Lives Matter" movement.

A ticket sporting two Alpha Males, moreover, is likely to infuriate the Alpha females of media (including those with the Y chromosome).

Noblesse Oblige

In an interview with NBC, Trump explained the difference between the politicians running and a businessman like himself: He has a lot to lose. They have nothing to lose.

As a longtime observer and analyst writing in opposition to the state and the political process, I find the specter of the anti-politician—the rugged, unrefined, cowboy individualist—fascinating, certainly worthy of tracking, and quintessentially American.

Among America's great industrialists and capitalists there has always been a long history of *noblesse oblige*—the notion that wealth, power and prestige carry responsibilities.

Trump Should Triangulate

Public service to the American Founders meant that men put their own fortunes and sacred honor on the line. Their lives too.

~August 7, 2015

5. TRUMP COULD SEND THE SYSTEM'S SYCOPHANTS SCATTERING

During the first primetime Republican debate, in Cleveland, Ohio, Donald Trump delivered the same slogans and failed to flesh out positions. While the man is quick and engaging; he came unprepared.

Ideas have not solidified Trump's success, but a powerful persona, true-blue patriotism and a willingness to put his substantial estate to the service of both. Trump now enjoys more support than he had prior to Cleveland, leading in national polls and in early voting states. Henpecked though he was by the "Murdoch Media's" golden goose—Megyn Kelly—Trump demonstrated that he is what his constituency craves: A man in the old mold. Trump is not an excuse for a man who'll bolt like so many rabbits when a couple of girls get in his face and grab his mic. I allude to socialist-in-Seattle Bernie Sanders (D), over whom two African-American women rode racial roughshod.

When members of the media pontificate that Trump's ascent reflects the base's disgust with the establishment, they fail to include themselves in that detested clique. To befuddle viewers and malign The Base, media even fib about who the establishment is.

Steve Hayes, senior writer for *The Weekly Standard*, a bastion of the Republican establishment, asserted on Fox

News that the Koch brothers of Koch industries, big bankers for the Republicans, are not of the establishment. Central to the media enterprise is a worldview that looks to the state and its stooges as the sole repository of the public good.

Donald Trump must be observed from the standpoint not of policy, but of process; as someone who could smash apart the political system and send its sycophants scattering to the four corners of the earth.

The establishment, Republican and Democrat, has a tendency to hunt in packs. Thus did compadre John King of the liberal network CNN offer a variation on the Goldberg theme: "The base wants to break all the glass."

Amid sneers about Trump's "crazy, entertaining, simplistic talk," the none-too bright Joan Walsh, Salon editor-in-chief, proclaimed (MSNBC): "I look at those people and I feel sad. That is really such a low common denominator. They're all Republicans ... they really don't have a firm grasp on reality."

For failing to foresee Trump's staying power, smarmy Michael Smerconish (CNN) scolded himself adoringly. He was what "Mr. Trump would call 'a loser.'" Smerconish's admission was a way of copping to his superiority. From such vertiginous intellectual heights, Smerconish was incapable of fathoming the atavistic instincts elicited by the candidate. Nevertheless, the broadcaster "quadrupled down." The country would be delivered from Donald by Mexican drug lord El Chapo, who'd scare Trump away.

Campbell Brown, another banal bloviator, ventured that Trump resonates with a fringe and was fast approaching a time when he would, like Herman Cain and Michele Bachmann, "max-out the craziness" quotient.

Trump supporters were simply enamored of his vibe, said a dismissive Ellis Henican.

As derisive, another Fox News commentator spoke about the "meat and potatoes" for which Trump cheerleaders hanker. I suspect he meant "red meat."

National Journal's Ronald Brownstein divined his own taxonomy of the Republican base beast: the "upscale Republicans and the blue-collar Republicans." The group of toothless rube-hicks Brownstein places in Trump's camp.

Like Megyn Kelly, pollster Frank Luntz stacks his focus groups with "regimists." According to Luntz' own brand of asphyxiating agitprop, the little people want to elect someone they'd have a beer with.

A British late night anchor—a CNN hire!—offered this non sequitur: Trump painting himself as anti-establishment and at the same time owning hotels: this was a contradiction. In the mind of this asinine liberal, only a Smelly Rally like "Occupy Wall Street" instantiates the stuff of rebellion and individualism. (Never mind that the Occupy Crowds were walking ads for the bounty business provides. The clothes they wore, the devices they used to transmit their sub-intelligent message; the food they bought cheaply at the corner stand to sustain their efforts—these were all produced, or brought to market by the invisible hand of the despised John Galts and the derided working class.)

Trump Could Send The System's Sycophants Scattering

I know not what exactly the oracular Krauthammer said to anger Trump, but it was worth it: "Charles Krauthammer is a totally overrated person ... I've never met him ... He's a totally overrated guy, doesn't know what he's doing. He was totally in favor of the war in Iraq. He wanted to go into Iraq and he wanted to stay there forever. These are totally overrated people."

Even media mogul Rupert Murdoch moved in on Trump, calling him an embarrassment to his friends and to the country.

Inadvertently, one media strumpet came close to coming clean about the serial failures of analysis among her kind. Wonkette, or Wonkette Emerita, aka Ana Marie Cox, spoke of "the superfluousness of the media's predictions and its inability to perform the service of making sense of events." Like Smerconish, Cox is hoping against hope that the *lumpenproletariat* are having fun at her expense and "are in some way in on the joke" that is Trump.

In case you think only liberals look down at the little people—by "liberals" I mean Democrats and Republicans—listen to Rand Paul's pronouncement on the mental midgets who find merit in Donald Trump:

"I think this is a temporary sort of loss of sanity. But we're going to come back to our senses and look for somebody serious to lead the country at some point."

~August 14, 2015

6. THE GOLDEN GOOSE THAT HENPECKED DONALD TRUMP

It's "R & R for Megyn Kelly," the Fox News Channel announced last week on its website, followed by a gooey note from Kelly herself. Why was FNC broadcasting the vacation schedule of the Golden Goose that henpecked Donald Trump? Had Kelly been licked into shape by Trump? Was she off to lick her wounds?

Since the testy exchange between Trump and Kelly, at the first prime-time Republican debate, in Cleveland, Ohio, the anchor's eponymous TV show, *The Kelly File*, has covered the meteoric rise of Mr. Trump sparingly. Perhaps Kelly has come to view herself as a kingmaker. Perhaps she thinks that should she choose not to report about a newsmaker; he'll somehow fade into obscurity.

Full disclosure: At first blush, I was impressed by the quality of Fox News' journalism, in Cleveland, writing too exuberantly that "the true stars of the debate were the ruthless, impartial, analytical" reporters. Better that Kelly be the one to ask foolish, fem-oriented questions of The Donald than future Dem moderators. It neutralizes the latter. Or so I reasoned.

Moreover, it's indisputable that compared to previous presidential debates overrun as they were by Democrat journos—Kelly, Bret Baier and Chris Wallace did a good job. No presidential debate should, however, be gauged by how it departs from debates in which questions such as these are posed:

"Senator Obama, how do you address those who say you're not authentically black enough?"

"Senator Dodd, you've been in Congress more than 30 years. Can you honestly say you're any different?"

"Congressman Kucinich, your supporters certainly say you are different. Even your critics would certainly say you are different ... What do you have that Senators Clinton and Obama do not have?" [Wait a sec. I know the answer: a trophy wife.]

And how about this intellectually nimble follow-up?

"Senator Clinton, you were involved in that [how-am-I-different] question. I want to give you a chance to respond [to that how-am-I-different question]."

"Senator Obama, you were also involved in that [how-am-I-different] question, as well. Please respond."

The final crushingly stupid question to the one-trick donkeys, debating in the 2007 CNN/YouTube Democratic presidential debate, was this:

"Who was your favorite teacher and why, Senator Gravel?"

The "journalist" pounding the presidential candidates was jackass Anderson Cooper of CNN.

Before she beat a retreat, Kelly had assembled a studio audience of Republican establishmentarian, to whom she directed another leading question: She herself knew nobody who'd call a woman a pig or a dog. Could they say the same? Kelly was alluding to the litany she had directed at Trump during her Cleveland performance (where she had cast herself as leading lady).

Kelly: "You've called women you don't like, 'fat pigs,' 'dogs,' 'slobs,' and 'disgusting animals.'"

Trump [in good humor]: "Only Rosie O'Donnell."

Megyn [bare-fanged]: "No it wasn't. For the record, it was well beyond Rosie O'Donnell. Your Twitter account has several disparaging comments about women's looks. You once told a contestant on 'Celebrity Apprentice' it would be a pretty picture to see her on her knees. Does that sound to you like the temperament of a man we should elect as president?"

Still under the brain-addling spell of the Cooper-Candy Crowley brain trust, I thought no less of Kelly for that dumbest of questions. Her anti-individualist, collectivist feminism is news to her fans, but not to me. Kelly's vocabulary is of a piece with the nauseating vocabulary of third-wave feminism.

More irksome was her allusion to the dignity of The Office. A while ago, fancy pants Kelly joined Don Lemon (CNN), Cooper and Rachel Mad Cow to editorialize angrily at Obama for damaging the dignity of The Office. These celebrity journos were, in fact, green with envy over GloZell Green, a YouTube sensation to whom president Obama granted an interview. Good for him.

Our TV narcissists—they live not for the truth, but for a seat at the Annual White House Sycophant's Supper, or alongside the smarmy Jon Stewart (or his unfunny South African replacement), or next to the titillaters of *The View*, or on the late-night shows—were jealous. Dented was the vanity of the egos in the anchor's chair.

A good president deserves respect. A bad one doesn't. This abstraction called "the presidency" is owed nothing. Having no respect for The Office, *per se*, I want Trump to continue to break stuff. Besides which the American presidency was pimped out a longtime ago—well before the current POTUS and FLOTUS held soirees sporting disco balls and the half-nude, pelvis-grinding Beyoncé.

Kelly herself has fast succumbed to the female instinct to show-off, bare skin, flirt and wink. She now also regularly motormouths it over the occasional smart guest she entertains (correction: the one smart guest, Ann Coulter). At the same time, Kelly has dignified the tinnitus named Dana Perino (former press secretary for President George W. Bush) with a daily slot as Delphic-oracle.

Trump, on the other hand, has proven he can be trusted to beat up on the right women.

Exhibit A is Elizabeth Beck, a multitasking "attorney," who once deposed Donald Trump while also waving her breast pump in his face, demanding to break for a breast-pumping session. "You're disgusting. You're disgusting," the busy billionaire blurted in disbelief.

And she was. Still is. Accoutered for battle, Beck recently did the rounds on the networks. In addition to a mad glint in the eye, Beck brought to each broadcast a big bag packed with milking paraphernalia.

Had she cared about boundaries and propriety, Kelly would have asked Trump how he kept his cool during a legal deposition, with an (ostensible) professional, who insisted on bringing attention to her lactating breasts.

Writes curmudgeon columnist Fred Reed, who regularly tracks our malevolent matriarchy's "poor sense of social boundaries":

> The United States has embarked, or been embarked, on a headlong rush into matriarchy, something never before attempted in a major country. Men remain numerically dominant in positions of power, yes, but their behavior and freedom are ever more constrained by the wishes of hostile women. The effects have been disastrous. They are likely to be more so. The control, or near control, extends all through society. Politicians are terrified of women. ... The pathological egalitarianism of the age makes it career-ending to mention that women in fact are neither equal nor identical to men. ...

Not quite in the league of Elizabeth Beck yet, Megyn Kelly was, nevertheless, in need of a dressing-down and a time-out.

~August 21, 2015

7. TRUMP'S REAGANESQUE MIC MOMENT

Donald Trump's brusque, plainspoken manner masks a fierce intelligence that should not be underestimated. Myself, I had experienced a momentary lapse in judgment with respect to the quality of Fox News Channel's journalism, during the first primetime Republican debate, in Cleveland, Ohio. Trump, on the other hand, was never blindsided by the nicely-packaged production that is Megyn Kelly. Kelly, in his plain and simple estimation, "was just not very good or professional."

Indeed, since returning from her post-spat "vacation," Kelly's Trump-free broadcasts have been flat. "Off her game," Trump tweeted out, right away. And while the celebrity anchor is still drawing ratings, this cannot last, absent the biggest news item: Donald Trump. I expected the anchor to come to her senses, and start working hard to get newsmaker Trump back on *The Kelly File*. This has yet to transpire.

Kelly's most recent belly flop came while "interviewing" Jorge Ramos, another celebrity newscaster who has been on the receiving end of Trump's much-needed, manly ministrations. Ramos works for the Univision network, catering to Hispanics. Although he poses as a reporter, in reality, Ramos is an identity politics activist. This celebrated mediocrity—Ramos made it as one of *Time's* "Most

Influential People"—crashed a Trump event, held on August the 25th, in Dubuque, Iowa. It was plain that the "ethnic activist" had materialized not to ask Trump a question; but to protest the candidate's positions and read him the riot act (in a kind of Pidgin English).

Democratic candidate Bernie Sanders was chased off a Seattle stage by two militant, "Black Lives Matter" movementarians. Ramos, the head honcho of the more-powerful, "Hispanic Lives Matter (Only)" movement, was staging a similar performance, this time against Trump. And Trump was having none of it.

As is his wont, Ramos began, Trump explained, "ranting and raving and screaming, like a madman, and honestly being very disrespectful to all the other reporters." I watched the Ramos rant on CNN. (FNC's ratings are fated to fall, if the network fails to carry future Trump events.) Trump's gloriously funny description was also factual. Whereas Kelly began her "Breaking Tonight" segment— what's that all about?—by "informing" her viewers that Ramos had been booted from the Trump news conference; hers was only half the truth.

And half-truths in journalism help perpetuate wholesale lies. The whole truth is that "a very emotional" Ramos— another terrific Trumpianism—was first scolded firmly and told, "Excuse me. Sit down. You weren't called. Sit down. Sit down." When Ramos continued to stomp about like the Brothers Grimm's Rumpelstiltskin—a masterful Trump, with no more than a nod of the head, had him escorted out.

Temporarily.

Ramos was given a much-needed time-out. (Stop, look, and listen, parents. If the nation's mothers and fathers want fabulous kids like Donald Trump's; they ought to try conducting themselves this way with their stroppy offspring.) What occurred thereafter is the Real Story—a story Kelly failed to tell her viewers. Trump was not only masterful, but fair to a fault.

But bear with me a little longer.

First: Most media outlets—from the conservative Drudge Report to the liberal Mediaite—alighted rather oddly on the fleeting and pathetic cross-examination to which Kelly subjected Ramos, during an interview that exemplified misleading journalism.

The headlines: "Megyn to Ramos: Why Would Trump Want to Talk to You?"

Such titles finesse Kelly's weasel words. The anchor whispered unconvincingly to Ramos: "Why would Trump want to engage with you when you are calling him the most hateful, divisive figure, running for president right now?" She then permitted Ramos to ramble on without once correcting his fibs. For Ramos was claiming that Trump The Dictator had silenced him and was therefore a threat to our very freedoms. He lied.

And Kelly let The Big Lie thread the entire segment.

Five minutes and nine seconds into the broadcast, almost imperceptibly, Kelly smuggled The Real Story into her sweetness-and-light exchange with Ramos:

"Even when you came back in ..."

That's the rub: During the Ramos-Trump mic moment, Trump was both magnanimous and Reaganesque (with reference to Ronald Reagan's 1980, "I am paying for this microphone" moment, in Nashua, New Hampshire). Once Ramos had calmed down (albeit to a blind panic), Mr. Trump invited him back in. The lengthy exchange Trump pursued with this malevolent moron—that was the "Breaking News" Kelly all but failed to mention.

The most modern political communicator in this field," "a great communicator," were the descriptives used by two hostile CNN commentators to characterize Trump's firm, forthright, masterful control of the Ramos wreck.

As this writer sees it, Trump was doing something much more modest and more valuable.

Common rules of procedure are as traditionally Anglo-American as they come. Instinctively did an ethnic agitator seek to sack a common American custom. As reflexively did Donald Trump move to restore a timeless, civilizing practice.

~August 28, 2015

8. TRUMP'S GOOD FOR THE ENGLISH LANGUAGE

When In The U.S. Or Britain, Speak English.

Donald Trump's retort to Jeb Bush's rattling off in Spanish on the campaign trail conjures an old joke told in Israel of my youth. It was aimed at the ultra-orthodox Jew who dresses weirdly and won't speak Hebrew. Here goes:

Walking down the street is a Sabra (a Jew born in Israel), clad in the pioneer's outfit of shorts and a Tembel Hat. ("Tembel" is Hebrew for silly. The "Tembel Hat" is cone-like headgear, utterly useless in providing protection from the merciless sun.) From across the street, in Yiddish—the language of the diaspora—an ultra-orthodox Jew clad in black garb shouts obscenities at the Sabra. The minuscule ultra-orthodox community believes that speaking Hebrew before Messiah arrives is heretic and will delay the coming of Messiah (also known as the longest coming in history). For Messiah to materialize, the Jew must remain weak, dispossessed and persecuted—a sickly spirit without a corporeal country to call his own.

The Israeli shouts back, "Speak Hebrew, goy!" Goy meaning non-Jew.

Trump took a jab at Jeb for using Spanish to dismiss the mogul's conservative credentials. Via CNN: "'I like Jeb,' Trump told Breitbart News. 'He's a nice man. But he should really set the example by speaking English while in the United States.'"

The Trumpian reference was to the former Florida governor's comments to reporters ... about Trump's policies. "'*El hombre no es conservador*,' Bush said, which translates to, 'This man is not a conservative.'"

Not only was Trump's visceral retort in defense of English righteous; it was also culturally conservative in the best of ways.

Restoring Truth To Language

Paraphrased, here is a collection of Trumpian straight-talk on the *Zeitgeist*. (Donald's "most notable insults," as *The Hill* would have it):

* We are led by stupid people. Very, very stupid people.

* Media are dishonest.

* Talking to Anderson Cooper is a waste of time.

* War-all-the-time Charles Krauthammer is an overrated, clueless clown.

* Anthony Weiner is the definition of a perv. (Or, as one Jewish writer you'll recognize put it, the "Weiner worm is a poster boy for anti-Semitism.")

* Elizabeth Beck is disgusting. [She's the wild-eyed attorney who turned a deposition of the busy businessman into a legal brief on breast-milk pumping.]

* The once-great *National Review* ... [Trump translated: NR is no longer great.]

* "George Bush sends our soldiers into combat, they are severely wounded, and then he wants $120,000 to make a boring speech to them?" [Yet another insight about Genghis Bush shared by yours truly, in a past blog post referring, in particular, to Bush charging the "Helping a Hero" charitable fund for speaking (in tongues) to their beneficiaries. First Bush sent these soldiers to die for nothing in Iraq and Afghanistan. Next he robbed those who came back broken.]

* Penn Jillette's show is terrible. [A self-evident truth.]

"Do we believe in the gene thing?" roared Trump at a crowd that had assembled to hear him speak in Mobile, Alabama, last month. Yes, he mentioned the G Factor. Trump was touting his genetic lineage; says he comes from a family of high-achievers. Hasn't the guy received *any* briefings on the prevailing linguistic Cultural Marxism—euphemized as political correctness—in the country he seeks to govern? It is an axiom of liberal establishmentarians like Jeb, George and the rest that the nature-nurture debate has been settled, politically, at least. According to liberal liturgy, of which Trump appears to know nothing; if not for largely exogenous circumstances—all human beings would be capable of similar accomplishments. Many a co-opted scientist will second the *political dictum* that there is no such thing as general intelligence. Speak, if you must, about the phenotype—even genotype—of all individual traits, but not intelligence. As for the possibility of group genotypic intelligence: Don't go there!

On America's conflict-of-interest riddled, corrupt press corps, Trump quipped: "Shouldn't George Will have to give a disclaimer every time he is on Fox News that his wife works for Scott Walker? (Walker briefly and unsuccessfully tested the presidential waters in 2015.)

That brings me back to the topic of intelligence, to which failed candidate Scott Walker relates as Trump relates to the tyranny of political correctness. In the course of vying for the Republican Party's nomination in the 2016 presidential election, the governor from Wisconsin came up with another "conservative," cogent idea: equal opportunity fencing. Reflexively—and laboring to show he does not discriminate against Mexico—Walker showed himself to be an indiscriminate bumpkin. Walker called building a wall along the border between the U.S. and Canada a "legitimate issue."

Illegal immigration and the security of the southern border with Mexico have been major issues in the Republican race for president, but the northern border has not been discussed. Mr. Walker made the comments in response to a question from a NBC News reporter. "That is a legitimate issue for us to look at," he said (BBC News).

Like the official Left, "conservatives" are in revolt against nature and reality. Canadian or Mexican; to the Bush and Walker egalitarian, the potential of all people is the same. Therefore all borders must be similarly defended or undefended. Does the U.S. have a problem with a deluge of illegal immigrants pouring over the Canadian border? No. Canada is a high-wage area. The U.S. is a high-wage area. Latin America is a low-wage area. Migratory pressure, Mr. Walker, flows from low-wage to high-wage regions; from the Third World to the First World, until migratory equilibrium is reached when First World becomes Third World.

Donald Trump's tone is unhelpful, Jeb Bush keeps sniveling in that soporific singsong of his. To the contrary. Not for nothing do our linguistic tormentors (like their communist-party mentors) seek to regulate language. For to be vested in linguistic accuracy is to be vested in the truth. The closer the language we use approximates reality—and, by extension, the truth—the greater the likelihood that our actions will follow.

In this sense, Trump's blunt, in-artful language is immensely helpful.

~September 18, 2015

9. DONALD, DON'T LET FOX NEWS ROGER AMERICA ... AGAIN

Bless Donald Trump. Inadvertently, by just being Donald, Mr. Trump has delivered more good news to liberty lovers.

In his bid for the presidency, Mr. Trump is not only threatening the Republican establishment, but is forcing a war with the cable news channel that does the Republican regimists' bidding. The Fox News Channel backed Genghis Bush's wars. The Powers That Be at FNC now wish to roger (Ailes) America, again, by delivering the country to neoconservative tool Marco Rubio, or to fool John Kasich (governor from Ohio), or to Ms. Fiorina, whom tacky media types call "Carly." However, this little lady's honeyed words conceal a burning desire to commit the country to an arms race with China and Russia.

Not for naught did Scott Walker go from two percent in the polls, to zero, to sayonara. Walker, that live wire, picked up his marbles and went home, blaming Trump for making him sad. But like the rest of the establishment's candidates, Walker had served up the same sub-intelligent, hackneyed lies about the root-causes of the migration problem plaguing Europe (Twitter hashtag #RapeFugees).

Syrian, Iraqi and Libyan populations are on the move, the neoconservative posse preaches, because of a failure to remove Bashar Hafez al-Assad, a man who was the source of stability in Syria, much like Saddam Hussein was in Iraq.

Have we learned nothing from the perils of toppling law-and-order dictators, only to see the rise of barbarians worse than their predecessors? Evidently not.

Bar Rand Paul and, to a degree Donald Trump, all the Republican candidates insist that American exceptionalism lies in leading the world not in technological innovation, comity, commerce and as exemplars of individual rights— but by projecting military power the world over. The U.S. government's bankruptcy, the candidates see as having no bearing on their own unanimous plans for an arms race with the other super powers and a renewed military offensive in the Middle East.

Since the second primary season Republican debate, at the Ronald Reagan Presidential Library, in California, FNC's Sean Hannity has been promoting Rubio's rabid ideation with zeal, replaying and praising on radio the neoconservative candidate's most militant, war-on-the-world lines. Rubio regularly trashes Vladimir Putin for trying to prop up Assad, so that the Islamic State does not capture Damascus. The very forceful Bill OReilly continues to profess admiration for the feeble Jeb Bush, who, poor thing, resembles a tiny pooch nipping at the heels of Donald Trump. Is this not due to Jeb's thoroughbred "invite the world; invade the world" neoconservatism?

Regrettably, other than to sensibly say that he'd get along with Putin, Trump made absolutely no attempt to demonstrate a familiarity with the issues, at Simi Valley. He might want to rethink his relaxed approach, for it belies the candidate's claim to have surrounded himself with the best people possible, or to have good judgement.

Trump's good judgment has since surfaced in a conversation with Greta Van Susteren: "If Putin goes into Syria and is "able to knock out ISIS," that's not the worst thing he's ever heard, Trump told the host. That excellent instinct—allow Putin to degrade and destroy ISIS if he wants to—comes from a very different perspective than the lamentations of Rubio-cum-Jeb-cum-OReilly over Russia "replacing us as the single most important power broker in the Middle East."

You see, Trump's instinct is to conduct foreign policy that benefits Americans. He doesn't want Americans dying for nothing. Rubio's prime objective is to conduct foreign policy that aggrandizes Washington. Like other neoconservatives, he dreads being a politician in a country that is no longer the world's military hegemon. For if America busies itself not with elective wars, but with commerce, the shift in power and prestige will be away from politicians who prosecute wars, and back to The People who produce prosperity.

"I'm owned by the people!" affirmed Trump, who wants what the people want. Having spent a total of two years of his working life outside government, Rubio—reflexively, not consciously—wants what'll glorify The State, the thing by which he survives and thrives.

And what does the battered GOP base want? The base, I hope, has wizened up to the neoconservatives.

The base, I hope, will realize that neoconservatives are still in the business of creating their own parallel reality and forcing ordinary Americans, Europeans and Middle-Easterners to inhabit the ruins. As I read it, the GOP base wants government to reverse the things it has done; to repeal laws, wars, and do no more harm.

Unless in defense of the realm, Americans are uninterested in more of the same foreign-policy folly. Let us keep our military mitts to ourselves, and defend our own borders. That, it would appear, is the prevailing sentiment among Republican voters, although not among the regimists who congregated at the Reagan Library.

Therefore, it is to Rand Paul's prescriptions during the debate that Trump should look, and not to the War Tourette's of the rest:

• Refrain from a rash foreign policy.
• Engage with Russia and China.
• Talk to the Mullahs before you "bomb, bomb, bomb, Iran" (a jingle popularized by jingoist John McCain).
• Leave dope policy to the states (not ideal, for consumption is to be left to the individual, but better than most).
• Do not sign on to bomb Assad out of existence. You'll miss him when he's gone.
• Remind Hillary Clinton who broke Libya.

Donald Trump has done another fine thing since Simi Valley, about which the media is audibly silent. In the honorable tradition Benjamin Franklin wished to establish, Trump said he'd forgo a salary as president. Many of our Founding Fathers believed America's representatives ought not to be paid at all.

As a man among metrosexuals, Trump's demeanor, naturally, is unlike that of his fork-tongued adversaries. Nevertheless, Trump was genial, even gracious, at Simi Valley. He showed contrition over his unkind cuts about Carly Fiorina's face. Fiorina could have cracked a smile, but didn't. (Or, perhaps she couldn't, considering the alleged and likely nips-and-cuts suffered by The Face).

And Trump refused to grovel. Good. Groveling about impolitic statements is the first sign of a housebroken GOPer.

So here's why Trump is good for liberty:

By waging internecine warfare against the political masters and their mouthpiece (Fox News Channel), Trump is undermining the bastions of neoconservatism in America; he is dealing a structural blow to the edifice of Beltway Republicanism.

In response, the Beltway boys are rising on their little hind legs.

As Megyn Kelly riffed about Trump's sexism, Fox News commentator Rich Lowry blurted out this on *Kelly's File*: "Carly Fiorina cut Trump's balls off with the precision of a surgeon." (Kelly, who is turning out to be rather vacuous, detected no sexism in Lowry's fit of words.) Another slick Republican strategist, Rick Wilson, a regular on CNN, recently asked Trump supporter Ann Coulter on Twitter if Trump paid her "more for anal."

Trump, for his part, fired first on the political flank. Now, in a pincer movement, he opened up a new front and is gunning for the establishment's media megaphone. This is why Trump's war with Fox News is part of a just, war of liberation.

~September 25, 2015

10. A HALLOWEEN HORROR STORY IN THE PEOPLE'S HOUSE

Washington is moving aggressively to inoculate itself against The Insurgents. By the looks of it, there might not be a Republican insurgency.

The series of political eruptions begun when Donald Trump appeared on the scene could be losing momentum. The Republican Comitatus —"the sprawling apparatus that encompasses" political party leaders, pseudo-intellectuals, media, donors and kingmakers— to use Cullen Murphy's description of Rome on the Potomac, has sprung into action to restore *status quo*.

Insider Paul Ryan has secured himself the position of House Speaker. Ask neoconservative kingpins William Kristol, John McCain, Roger Ailes and the Koch Brothers who they'd tap for the position, any position—and the Ryan/Marco Rubio duo would be the reply.

Senator Marco Rubio, however, is just where the vampiric Republican regimists want him: running his mouth off in the presidential debates. Paul Ryan is thus the right young blood to rein in a rebellion dominated by an older and wiser America.

Incidentally, neoconservative tool Rubio brought up some bad memories, during a September, Fox News broadcast, when he called for a "new American century," an impetus that elicited a Halloween shudder. The Project for the New American Century (PNAC) consisted of a group of prominent global interventionists close to or in the administration of Bush II. This group—among whom were neoconservatives Dick Cheney, Donald Rumsfeld and Paul Wolfowitz—had formulated a scheme for a post-Hussein Iraq well before September 11. By the early summer of 2001, Bush had assembled his neocon posse whose plan to go global could, at the time, be found on the Project for the New American Century's website.

But I digress (or maybe not).

According to historian Clement Wood, it is an unwritten law followed "scrupulously," "although omitted from the Constitution," that the Speaker of the House of Representatives possesses "the czar-like power" "to recognize only such members as he pleases, and thereby strongly to influence legislation."

After playing hard to get, pampered prima donna Paul Ryan agreed to assume the czar-like powers of Speaker of the House.

Much media coverage was given over to young Ryan's feminist-worthy demand for a work-life balance. It certainly got the girls on CNN hot, Andy Cooper, in particular. (Try telling a major, private American corporation you want the same. You'll be told in deeds more so than in words that you can have your bloody work-life balance, but expect to remain at the same grade till you retire, or are nudged into retirement on account of your love of equilibrium.)

But that's OK. Political work is wealth-destroying work. The less of it Ryan does; the better.

Lost in the victory Ryan scored with feminists was the blow he dealt to the Republican insurgency rising.

As a rule, younger Republicans seem to want government to facilitate diversity, dope and gay marriage (none of which were in the Constitution). The older generation wants its leave-me-alone rights (in the Bill or Rights) restored.

Grand Old Party oldies are more likely to want less government than the youngsters they sired.

Duly, old school Tim Huelskamp, Republican representative from Kansas, who had been bullied by outgoing Speaker John Boehner for defying the speaker, told *The Washington Examiner* that no other speaker he knew of "would ... have as much power as Paul Ryan asked for himself":

"Those conditions include a request that the House eliminate a rule that allows a member to seek a vote to oust the speaker. That provision is part of the original rules of the House, authored by Thomas Jefferson."

Ryan haggled until his anti-Jeffersonian "conditions" were met. These were, confirmed *Time* magazine, that he "emerge as House Republicans' unity candidate, endorsed by the three major factions of House Republicans."

The Freedom Caucus folded.

In the Jeffersonian tradition, the most conservative of lawmakers wanted to be able to dissent from leadership without being censured by the speaker. In the tradition of "Boehner of Orange," whom the Left has just about beatified, Ryan wished to further consolidate power in the office of speaker.

The Ryan, regimist takeover had been presaged by a promising coup in the People's House, earlier in October. Another Boehner boy, House Majority Leader Kevin McCarthy, was considered a shoo-in for the position of speaker. One minute McCarthy was there, the next minute he was ... gone. The magic began with another, older Republican called Walter Jones. Representative Jones, who is in the habit of signing off humbly as "Walter," terrified the Californian Republican, Kevin McCarthy, into withdrawing his bid for speaker.

"Walter" did his magic by circulating a missive in which he urged, nay demanded, that "any candidate for Speaker of the House, majority leader, and majority whip, withdraw himself from the leadership election if there are any misdeeds he has committed ..."

No one knows or much cares why McCarthy recused himself with a speed that made the zombie media come alive. But CNN's Dana Bash and her zombie fellow travelers on network and cable confessed to being flabbergasted.

McCarthy's magic disappearing act was a feat unseen before. The predictable hustle-and-flow of political pimping had been disrupted. ("Walter": Come out and take a bow. The reason nobody has thanked this patriot is likely because "Walter"—unlike his wicked party members—has tried to atone for destroying Iraq.)

McCarthy was likely fooling around with fellow Representative Renee Ellmers. More important: He would have screwed-over the conservative caucus rising.

So, Kevin was gone. His departure so unusual did not portend chaos in the ranks, as the mono-cultural media insisted. Rather, it was a harbinger of creative destruction.

Enter Paul Ryan. As pretty as Damien—down to the shiny black hair and piercing blue eyes—the man was equal to the task of restoring the rule of Boehner.

"What Edmund Burke said about the House of Commons in his day applies in spades to a House packed with the likes of Speaker Ryan. 'Designed as a control for the people,' the House has become a control 'upon the people.'"

The Republican Comitatus, like the Democratic praetorians, has a media flank. And Fox News' Megyn Kelly had moved into shooting position. As mentioned in the Introduction, the anchor was first to galvanize the GOP's biggest guns, in her crusade against the one anti-establishment Republican candidate who dared call her bluff (and expose her fluff).

Kelly's love-in with Emperor Charles Koch exemplified the Barbara Walters School of saccharine, sell-out "journalism." The Kelly woman's clucking and cooing on that occasion was as disgraceful as it was dumb: She solicited one unflattering, hackneyed condemnation after the other about Mr. Trump.

Hard on Kelly's Jimmy Choo heels came the *Wall Street Journal*, another progressive wing of the GOP establishment, featuring a highly contrived Koch-centric article in which "ordinary voter" Charles Koch sounded off against Trump's so-called intolerant "tone." (Yes, borders are an outrageous intolerance, as is the notion of the pre-eminence of English in American life.)

The Koch Brothers are a GOP Goliath worth around $115 billion. They're gunning for Donald Trump who's worth $10 billion.

The stars in the Republican establishment's constellation were aligning against the insurgent.

~October 30, 2015

11. WHAT TRUMP'S UP AGAINST: IN THE WEST, THE INMATES RUN THE ASYLUM

"Hey, it's me, Salah Abdeslam. Did you see the attacks across Paris? *Inshallah*, may we have many more like them. Brothers Brahim Abdeslam, Abdelhamid Abaaoud, myself and others pulled it off. I'm still in Paris. I need a ride back to Brussels. Come get me or send an Uber driver."

After executing 130 people in Paris, on November 13, and maiming many more, Abdeslam called his compadres in Belgium to ask for a lift home. I can't vouch for the precise wording of the telephonic exchange between terrorist Salah Abdeslam and his contacts in Belgium. But the call took place, as BBC News reported, on November 26. And it must have been quite a relaxed one, circumstances considered.

Still on the lam, Abdeslam knows he has nothing to fear. The French authorities were on heightened alert. The Kufar's (unbeliever) telephones had all been tapped. Yet Salah's faith in the French fools was unshaken for a reason. Without court orders, as *The Guardian* tells it, François Hollande's socialist government taps phones and emails, hacks computers, installs "secret cameras and recording devices in private homes"; infects French Internet and phone service providers with "complex algorithms" designed to "alert the authorities to suspicious behavior."

What Trump's Up Against: In The West, The Inmates Run The Asylum

Yet it all—the French Surveillance State—amounts to naught.

Like gun laws, spy laws oppress only law-abiding, harmless individuals. As in all western democracies, France's Big Brother surveillance apparatus is as useless as it is oppressive.

France's "protectors" knew nothing of the conversations taking place under their noses. Duly, Marine Le Pen would be summoned to appear in Court for "inciting religious hatred against Muslims," in October 2015. Leader Le Pen, who loves her countrymen and would never harm them, was in court for saying "France for the French."

Yes, Salah knew all too well—still knows—that offensive speech French authorities would diligently prosecute, all the more so when uttered by a "white supremacist." But a suspicious looking swarthy supremacist like himself, hellbent on killing his hosts, would not so much as be stopped for an inquisitive chat.

Not on returning from one of many round trips to Syria and back, to Turkey and back, to Morocco and back. And not on returning to the scene of the crime.

Megyn Kelly, whose professional conduct has been utterly unbecoming—it's becoming more like Bawbawa Walter's journalistic porn by the day—took up an entire segment of her Fox News extravaganza to kibitz about the un-Islamic lifestyle of the architect of the attacks. OMG! Abdelhamid Abaaoud had been swilling whiskey in Paris' Saint-Denis district, in contravention of Islamic law, moaned Imam Kelly.

The real "breaking news" story Kelly missed.

Abaaoud was thus relaxing and celebrating *a day after* the successful attacks. *Shortly after* the attacks, Abaaoud had managed to return undisturbed to the scene of the crime to mill about among the moronic French gendarmes and survey his handiwork with them.

The "breaking news" here, Ms. Kelly, is the criminally negligent, worse-than-shoddy French police work.

Where were the roadblocks? Where was the rational profiling at the roadblocks? Where was the basic police procedure that used to see cops stop and politely question loiterers at a crime scene? Nowhere!

Thus did Paris' chief gendarme order the city's peaceful Jews to cancel public Hanukkah celebrations. Better that, than stop a North-African looking chap for a chat. Jews may be removing themselves from Paris' Public Square, but not Jihadis. Rest assured: With the help of their political and constabulary enablers, Jihadis are already surveying the city for more soft targets, just like the Parisian headquarters of Charlie Hebdo, a satirical newspaper, whose writers were exterminated in January of 2015.

France is no civilized outpost; it is paradise on earth for Muhammad's martyrs; it's hell on earth for their *dhimmis*.

Why, just the other day a Jewish teacher was stabbed in Marseilles by purported ISIS supporters. And a local businessman was beheaded near the city of Grenoble by two of Muhammad's acolytes, celebrating Ramadan with an act of Islamic conquest. These French Muhammadans brazenly impaled the poor man's severed head on a fence.

What Trump's Up Against: In The West, The Inmates Run The Asylum

Only the U.S. Transportation Security Administration employs more un-vetted Muslims than the French. According to *The Australian*, at least "57 workers with access to runways and aircraft were on [a French] intelligence watchlist as potential Islamist extremists."

One of the assailants at Bataclan, Omar Ismail Mostefai—mercifully, he blew himself to smithereens likely because he knew the gendarmes would take pity on him and slow down his journey to Gehenna—was fingered back "in 2010 as a suspected Islamic radical. Since then, Mostefai appears to have been able to travel to Syria; he may have also spent time in Algeria," attested BBC News.

Another Bataclan alumnus, Samy Amimour, a 28-year-old Frenchman, also partook in France's generous, frequent-flyer terrorist tours. He scuttled to commune with ISIS in Syria without being kept out of France, or deported for good to ISIS Land.

Still did a BBC News headline ask: "Paris attacks: Is bashing Belgium justified?"

An unqualified yes is the answer—provided blame is apportioned between France, Germany, The Netherlands and other European countries, which all keep the revolving door in operation, so that their Muslim youngsters may circumambulate from Europe to ISIS Land and back again.

When the butcher aforementioned, Brahim Abdeslam, commenced his pilgrimage to Syria, the Turks were sharp enough and responsible to send him packing back to Brussels, where he was wanted, but not a Wanted Man.

The best I kept for last: Salah Abdeslam was stopped by police "in his car," not once, but "three times in the hours following the attacks, on the last occasion near the Belgian border" (BBC News). Abdeslam and two fellow travelers were waved by, because they did not resemble Ms. Marine Le Pen.

To the presence of ISIS *in France*, the little man in charge of the country responded by dropping bombs *in Syria*. Hollande's lunacy excited neoconservatives stateside no end. That's because the inmates are running the American and European asylums, where The People are the real refugees.

Patriots who promise no more than to make the West safe for its people again; the gilded traitor elite threatens with court orders served upon them by Jihadis.

Marine Le Pen's Front National, the Freedom Party of Austria, and Geert Wilders' Party for Freedom, to be joined, indubitably, by Donald Trump, are outsiders in their homelands. But in France, it's business as usual for the barbarians.

~December 4, 2015

12. REDUCING MURDER-BY-MUSLIM IN THE HOMELAND

Right after the Murder-by-Muslim of the San Bernardino 14, on December 2, immigration lawyers peppered the press with praise for America's fiancé K-1 visa program. This immigration program is "robust" came the message from the lobbyists.

Onto this rickety scaffolding stepped the attorneys for *The Fockers*, I mean the Farooks. The family that spawned the assassins, and warned no one, was smart enough to hire proxies who spoke for the Ummah (the entire Islamic Nation). The two put on a masterful display of *taqqiya* (deception in furtherance of Islam), demanding what the American political class had authorized them to demand: Attach no culpability to Islam. Give "the alleged shooters" the benefit given to victims of religious bullying.

The Muslim-Media-Congressional complex was poised to make suitably weepy statements and move on. Death by Jihadis was just one of those things the little people would have to endure in "a free society." This, too, was the attitude of the asses warming the anchor's chair in TV newsrooms. We'll show the grief; we'll slobber suitably with the aggrieved, we'll lead with the most emotional clichés about the dearly departed, and on we'll go to the next news story. Any change in the *status quo* would be contrary to "our values."

Such is life: *C'est la vie*, so long as it doesn't happen to me.

In effect, the politicians committed to do nothing to reduce the exposure of America to the source of death. No domestic policy changes in the homeland have been floated. Promises aplenty, however, are being made to "carpet bomb" faraway lands as the solution to the "problem" in our land.

Enter Donald Trump.

The Collateral-Damage Calculus

Mr. Trump appears genuinely outraged by this crass and cruel political calculus. Trump was not going along with the notions implicit in the strategies proposed by the administration and the colluding political duopoly. These are that we trade a few American lives, every so often, in return for getting to brag about America's commitment to "freedom," our "open society," all the intangible nostrums our overlord in D.C. instruct us to celebrate.

Mr. Trump was not OK with the idea that mass murder by Muslim, every now and then, was the price of "our tolerance." Trump's visceral response seems odd to the political class and their media barnacles because it's the reaction of a regular, clear-thinking individual who has yet to be broken in by Washington.

If you're a Jihadi who's traveled to train abroad— American, permanent resident or anything else—"you are never-ever coming back into the U.S.," vowed Trump.

Having suggested the same a few months back in the essay, "A Modest Libertarian Proposal: Keep Jihadis OUT, Not IN," I would venture that immigration is a political grant of privilege; there is no natural right to immigrate into the U.S., not least if you are fixing to kill your coworkers.

Later, Trump followed up with a more radical statement; radical from a political perspective. He "called for a total and complete shutdown of Muslims entering the United States until our country's representatives can figure out what is going on":

> According to Pew Research, among others, there is great hatred towards Americans by large segments of the Muslim population. Most recently, a poll from the Center for Security Policy released data showing 'twenty-five percent of those polled agreed that violence against Americans here in the United States is justified as a part of the global jihad' and fifty-one percent of those polled, 'agreed that Muslims in America should have the choice of being governed according to Shariah.'

"Without looking at the various polling data," stated Mr. Trump, "it is obvious to anybody the hatred is beyond comprehension. Where this hatred comes from and why we will have to determine. Until we are able to determine and understand this problem and the dangerous threat it poses, our country cannot be the victims of horrendous attacks by people that believe only in Jihad, and have no sense of reason or respect for human life."

Squandering Vs. Conserving Scarce Resources

To grasp why Trump would counsel something so practical, yet so politically improper, one has to understand Trump the businessman. Good businessmen are programmed differently than politicians. As a gifted entrepreneur, Trump is averse to squandering scarce resources, money or manpower. As of October, 2015, for instance, "Trump had only put $2 million of his own cash into his campaign," against Jeb Bush's $28.9 million. The *Washington Post* marveled unnecessarily at "Donald Trump's extremely fiscally conservative campaign."

Politicians (and those who peddle them like the WaPo) do not understand the natural economic reality of scarcity. They control the production of money for their promiscuous purposes and they exert power over millions of interchangeable people in their territorial jurisdiction.

To a politician, fourteen lives in 322 million is a small price to pay for "our freedoms." Trump's political rivals look at the price exacted by a Muslim like Syed Farouk and his bride in the aggregate. Fourteen dead is not a steep price to pay for unfettered immigration from Islamic countries, peddled politically as "our values," "our tolerance," "our greatness."

This callous calculus is second nature to politicians like Lindsey Graham or Darth Vader Cheney. Not to Trump. "This must stop. We can't have this," he roared.

See, statistics are funny things. Insignificant probabilities, in this case an attack on each one of us, are immaterial unless they happen to YOU or ME. It is this calculus that politicians peddle. They rely on the fact that we'll adopt their sloganeering because each one of us is unlikely to die by Muslim.

But to do nothing stateside, as Trump's rivals imply, is to accept that lives lost are, in the grand scheme, insignificant.

The opposite is true for Trump. Taking losses offends his sensibilities. Trump, the consummate businessman, abhors and is angered by the preventable squandering of scarce assets: American lives. (Yes, Trump is an American Firster.) The death of a few Americans pains Mr. Trump, something that cannot be said about Obama, Hillary, Bernie or any of the insider GOPers.

How can you tell? The politicians—Rubio, Ryan—offer up platitudes; political niceties to excite the asses in the anchor's chair. They propose nothing to stop the slaughter, stateside. Instead, they demand a leap of faith—that you believe dropping "daisy cutters" on Muslims in the Middle East (only on the bad ones, naturally) will reduce the danger to Americans at home.

The instincts of private enterprise and politics; never the twain shall meet. Private-enterprise driven considerations are aimed at conserving, not squandering, scarce resources. If it loses an asset, the Trump Organization hurts.

In Politics, 'Nothing Succeeds Like Failure'

The second thing a businessman must do—a trait so obviously ingrained in Trump—is solve "The Problem." In Trump's universe, solving problems is ineluctably tied to the greater goals of realizing profits and growing the organization. ("Making America Great.")

The opposite is true in politics. You don't solve problems; you let them fester. Politically, problems are not all bad. Plunge the people into crisis, and they are likelier to fall prey to state schemes. Politicians accrue power over people in crisis.

"War is the health of the State," said a good progressive Randolph Bourne (1918). Never let a serious crisis go to waste," said bad progressive Rahm Emanuel. Both men understood the dynamics of state control. The first warned against it; the second capitalized on it.

Trump talks about taking practical, focused steps to reduce the murder by Muslim of Americans in the homeland. The politicians speak of abstractions; upholding our values, blah, blah—gibberish Trump is genetically incapable of uttering. For the "Our Values" Speak is meant to addle the mind; shame individuals into believing they are evil if they don't adopt the liberal pluralist faith put forward by all those who ride at the king's bridle, Republican and Democrat.

~December 11, 2015

13. NEUTRALIZING NEOCONSERVATIVE WAR TOURETTE'S

Donald Trump strode into the gaudy Venetian, in Las Vegas, for the CNN-Facebook Republican presidential debate, with a primary lead for the history books. As *Weekly Standard* put it, "Trump's lead over his primary opponents is larger than both Ronald Reagan's was in the 1980 race, and George H. W Bush's was in the 1988 contest." Not that you'd know it from the media's Trump-In-Decline School Of Alternate Reality, but "on a national level, Trump is clearly in a stronger position than Hillary Clinton is."

So, while Trump's debate was meaty on meaning; thin on policy—"our country doesn't win anymore. We don't win on trade. We don't win on the military. We can't defeat ISIS. We're not taking care of our great people, the veterans—the candidate was comfortably presidential and graciously conciliatory to the knaves of the Republican National Committee who've been plotting to thwart a Trump nomination from the inception.

Yet humbly did Trump profess his total commitment "to the Republican Party."

> I feel very honored to be the front runner. And I think I'll do very well if I'm chosen. If I'm so fortunate to be chosen, I think I'll do very well.

Polls have come out recently saying I would beat Hillary. I will do everything in my power to beat Hillary Clinton, I promise you.

So it is hoped that by professing his great respect for the Republican brass in Vegas, Trump has not let down his guard or "sold out."

Other than the conciliatory tone, there were no surprises about Trump's performance at "the final Republican debate before the election year begins." The lines—"We either have a country or we don't have one, I want a strong border and a wall, walls work, ask the Israelis"—all worked for the umpteenth time.

Touchingly Trumpian, too, was the, "I don't want our country to be taken away from us, and that's what's happening. The policies that we've suffered under other presidents have been a disaster for our country. We want to make America great again. And Jeb [Bush], in all fairness, he doesn't believe that."

The early, second-tier Republican performers remained hopelessly afflicted with War Tourette's, even spoiling for skirmishes with Russia. Governor Mike Huckabee distinguished himself by coming closer than all contenders in seriously commenting about Islam: "[Our job] is not to protect the reputation of Islam. It is to protect Americans first and foremost."

Both Dr. Ben Carson and Senator Ted Cruz may have believed themselves to be brave when they repeated the term "radical Islamic terrorism." Uttering it is supposed to signal seriousness about terrorism, in Republican circles. It signals confusion.

The mouthful, "radical Islamic terrorism," is itself an error because it's a redundancy. Islam is radical. It has never undergone a reformation. Most Muslims do not act on their radical religion, but the authentic, un-reformed Islam is dormant in the faithful. As a protected, parasitical class, politicians are bereft of the survivalist skills that have allowed our prehistoric ancestor Homo erectus to stick around long enough to turn into Homo sapiens. Donald Trump is not thus afflicted. Judging from the simple, sentient utterances on matters Muslim, Mr. Trump has no difficulty constructing mental categories of danger and using these as predictive—and protective—measures in the cause of the common man's safety.

Gratitude is owed to moderator Wolf Blitzer for reminding the likes of Senator Lindsey Graham, who yelled his yearning for George Bush—that after 9/11, it was "W" who told the nation that Islam was peace. Predictably, Graham, who polls a steady zero percent with Americans, maintained his lead with the news nitworks. More than anyone at the kiddy dais, Graham's fulminations excited the dark desires of CNN "analyst" Gloria Borger. Women love an energetic regime changer.

Another neoconservative, Senator Marco Rubio, became the object of Rand Paul's barbs. The Rand Rubio offensive was wise and well-rewarded. Alas, Rand, who shone during the debate, forgot to back off Donald Trump. Who knows? If Rand stops nipping at The Donald's heels, Trump might give the little guy a position as Secretary of State, in charge of foreign policy. And that would be a good thing.

On the foreign policy front, an alliance emerged that saw Trump, Paul and Cruz briefly unite to advance an America First foreign policy, and to volubly oppose the foreign policy forays of Rubio aka Genghis Bush aka Dick Cheney aka Jeb Bush aka John Kasich aka Carly Fiorina.

Thus when Chris Christie—who also shares the ideological cockpit with the neoconservatives—vowed to down Russian planes if they crossed a no fly zone he'd establish in Syria; Paul was quick to interject: "There's your candidate to start World War III."

"If we want to defeat terrorism, the boots on the ground need to be Arab boots on the ground," insisted Senator Paul splendidly. Then he went and spoiled it all by saying something stupid like, "If we ban Muslim immigration, the terrorists will have won."

"The terrorists win if Americans don't do as the politicians say" is reverse psychology and cliché rolled into one. The prez also keeps saying, "Dare do x, y or z on matters Muslim, and you guarantee that ISIS wins." Or, "ISIS wants you to do x, y, and z."

First, how do these asses know what ISIS wants? Or, are Barack Obama and Senator Paul simply ass-uming they know? It is more likely the two politicians are using reverse psychology to get Americans to comply with their own wishes.

In any event, if ISIS wants you, America, to do what in your estimation is best for you–perhaps ISIS is right and the president is wrong. Perhaps ISIS is right and Rand Paul is wrong. So, Senator Paul, we'll take that long moratorium on Muslim immigration. It's a winner for Americans. If ISIS approves, too, so be it. ISIS is happy; we are happy; everybody is happy; we all win.

After being set up for a confrontation, Both Trump and Cruz refused to beat up on each other. CNN moderator Dana Bash looked dejected, but was infinitely better behaved and more able than Fox News' Megyn Kelly had been at the first-ever debate. (Last night, Kelly tweeted out Cruz's coded anodyne assurances to moms: "I will do everything necessary to keep our children safe." Fuck the kids, Kelly. We're trying to have an adult conversation, here. Adult lives matter, too.)

Speaking of a drone, Ms. Fiorina failed to get past her funereal introduction: I beat breast cancer. I buried a child. I began as a secretary. I was called a bitch. Oy!

To sum: A vital node in the neoconservative network, Marco Rubio, was exposed for his open-borders record and odious alliance with Democrat Chuck Schumer with whom Rubio formed the Schubio Gang of Eight.

In their rosy post-debate analysis, Rubio's fans at Fox News failed to note how he stumbled further into incoherence by insisting a moratorium on Muslim immigration was unconstitutional. Not according to constitutional scholar Peter J. Spiro, who wrote in the *New York Times* that, "Trump's anti-Muslim plan is awful. And constitutional."

Trump would have "plenary power" to protect Americans from the sporadic but predictable eruptions of the Islamic faithful. Such exclusion of or dissociation from Islam's practitioners would approximate a defensive act, more commensurate with the libertarian non-aggression axiom than the military adventurism beloved by Democrats and neoconservatives alike.

Ultimately, 2016 will all come down to the only candidate who uttered the following plain but poignant passage:

"I feel a very, very strong bind, and really I'm bound to this country."

~December 18, 2015

14. TRUMP'S INVISIBLE, POOR WHITE ARMY'S WAITING ON THE ROPES

Donald Trump's mortal enemies in mainstream politics and media have shifted strategy. In the ramp-up to the Iowa caucuses, February 1, the culprits have been pushing presidential hopefuls Ted Cruz and Marco Rubio onto a defiant Republican base. The Cartel has taken to discussing Trump as a nightmare from which they'll soon awaken. Candidate Trump's energetic, politically pertinent speeches, and near daily rallies—packed to the rafters with supporters—are covered by media only to condemn this or the other colorful altercation. Ted Cruz, we're being lectured, is poised to topple Trump in Iowa.

But what do you know? On the eve of January 12, Trump punched through the lattice of lies, as if in recoil to the concentrated toxicity of Barack Obama's last State of Disunion address, featuring the divisive Nikki Haley in the GOP's corner. The media-political-complex was caught trousers down again. National polls had Trump at thirty-six percent, Reuters at thirty-nine percent. A CBS/NYT poll placed him seventeen points ahead of Ted Cruz, his closest rival. In Iowa, Trump leads Cruz twenty eight to twenty six percent.

The central conceit that currently defines media's self-serving surmises is that the Trump revolution is confined to the Right and is thus self-limiting. While the Right is always more courageous in bucking sclerotic authority, the Trump revolution isn't exclusively Republican or rightist. As *The Atlantic* cautioned, the polls are underestimating Trump's support. The slow kids of media have yet to discover the methodological flaws inherent in survey methodology. Subjects are more likely to reply truthfully in anonymous, online surveys than in face-to-face or telephonic questionnaires. As if to confirm that Trumpites are coming out of the closet, a January 13, YouGov.com poll, courtesy of the *Washington Examiner*, catapulted Mr. Trump to near fifty percent.

Something else has made the special-needs media boil with bile: It's the role of America's much-maligned, white majority—sixty-five percent and rapidly declining—in Trump's meteoric ascent. Trump's supporters are disenfranchised whites, left, right and center (or in an ideological no-man's land). The silent majority that dare not speak its name—other than to flagellate for collective sins and perceived privilege—is still the largest demographic bloc in the U.S.

Working class whites, in particular, have been led down a political *cul-de-sac*.

Omitted at last year's November 10, Fox Business, presidential debate were two loudly whispered secrets. The one was Marco Rubio's expensing the Republican Party for personal spending. The other: Terrifying data that a large segment of white America was ... dying. "Mortality among middle-aged Americans with a high-school degree or less increased by 134 deaths per 100,000 people between 1999 and 2013," wrote Olga Khazan of *The Atlantic*.

Mortality among working-class white Americans has risen by half a percent a year. "That means half a million people are dead who should not be dead." Since these whites are dying from "suicide, alcohol and drug poisonings, and alcohol-related liver disease," Khazan concluded sadly that "middle-aged white Americans are dying of despair." Otherwise, nobody has probed deeper than to advance reductive economic and educational causes.

My sense is that, "while Americans in their fifties and forties don't have enough money saved for retirement," there's more afoot than money. Most of us have come across emaciated, gaunt, poor white men and women in our communities; middle-aged, often younger whites standing on the curb, begging for change. Indeed, we members of the informal, White Lives Matter movement notice that poor whites in America are very badly off. But a political whiteout prohibits the candid discussion of their plight.

Unless they're being dubbed throw-away racists, bigots, or has-beens who can't let go of white privilege—white, working-class America is invisible. It has been so for decades.

Consider what befell Martin O'Malley, Democrat for president, at the Netroots Nation conference, in Phoenix. "Black lives matter, black lives matter," chanted activists at O'Malley, who dared to respond with the catchphrase, "Black lives matter. White lives matter. All lives matter." The maniacal reaction to O'Malley's truism was so vociferous, that soon he and the Democrats were denouncing the notion that all lives mattered, and apologizing to blacks for daring to imply that white lives mattered, too. A weak Bernie Sanders was practically chased off a Seattle stage by two "Black Lives Matter" women, and has since been silent about poor whites, except to promise proxy wars on Wal-Mart and Wall Street.

Politically, at least, white lives are forfeit.

Bernie is full of humanist bromides. The Democrat candidate's immigration plank, however, is "humane" to migrants and inhumane to their poor white American hosts. Sanders managed to discuss the plight of working class white America with MSNBC's Chris Hayes, without once mentioning immigration. Or the decimation of the coal industry in West Virginia, courtesy of Obama policies that saw 332 coal mines shuttered. These working-class white men came to D.C. hard hats in hand, to beg for their jobs. Nobody listened until Trump.

Stuff happens, poor whites are told. Quit being racist.

If you're working-class and white, you're invisible. You have been for decades. You used to be the backbone of the economy. No more. You're still the backbone of the U.S. military, more likely to die in the service of The State in far-flung countries. Your love of country is sanctioned provided it is confined to dying in the wars launched by Rome-on-the-Potomac.

You may find belonging only by risking your life abroad in the service of strangers, or opening your home to them, stateside. If you survive the combat-to-coffin career path,

Trump's Invisible, Poor White Army's Waiting On The Ropes

your love of community will need to encompass a million immigrants, each and every year, who'll have the run of your schools, hospitals, libraries, parks and workplace. Destined to fight against subsistence farmers in foreign lands, you find yourself harassed on your homesteaded land, at home, never free from federal aggression.

As a share of America's adult population, Donald Trump's invisible, poor white army likely forms less than forty-eight percent. To them could be added other whites who favor borders and hanker after closely-knit communities and such Burkean peculiarities. I would imagine the notorious Hammond and Bundy ranching families, fighting federal incursion in Nevada and Oregon, are eager to hear from the one candidate who has not called them terrorists.

This large, mostly white cohort is waiting on the ropes for … Donald Trump.

~January 15, 2016

15. TRUMP'S PROMISE TO NULLIFY LAWS

Former Fox News Channel broadcaster Glenn Beck, now of The Blaze TV, has been warning theatrically of an inchoate catastrophe should the country choose Donald J. Trump "as its next president." Trump "will be a monster much, much worse" than Barack Obama, says Beck.

Worse than George W. Bush? Will Trump be worse than the 43rd president, who is ranked 37th by Ivan Eland, author of *Recarving Rushmore: Ranking the Presidents on Peace, Prosperity, and Liberty?* In Eland's near-exhaustive appraisal, Bush II falls in the category of "bad," for having "undermined the Republic at home and abroad with interventionist policies," policies Trump has criticized. Stumping for Trump, former governor of Alaska Sarah Palin has taken pains to praise Rand Paul's libertarian recommendations that Jihadists be left to "duke it out" alone in the Middle East.

President Obama is a dreadful cur. About that Beck's correct. Like Bush, Obama has made it into the "bad" presidential category. But whereas Obama allowed Hillary to henpeck him into destabilizing one country, Libya; Bush Jr. gave the world the Iraq-Syria Axis of ISIS. Ranked 34th on the measures of peace, prosperity and liberty, the 44th president is "only a slightly improved version of George Bush."

The charismatic Ronald Reagan, the man "conservatives have enshrined as a demigod," was certainly as forceful as Donald Trump. Reagan was also remarkably perceptive in his anti-communist oratory. The "evil empire" appellation was as catchy as it was warranted. But face it; "tear down this wall, Mr. Gorbachev" didn't bring down the Soviet empire. Neither was Communist Russia crushed by Reagan's exorbitant "Star Wars fantasy of space-based missile defense." Rather, Communist Russia collapsed under the weight of a centrally planned economy (the kind brainiac Bernie Sanders and his supporters are eager to usher in).

Those of us who love Number 40 for his ability to express the immutably true principles of liberty and free-market capitalism must face the facts. While Elan loses some credibility in ranking Reagan *after* Obama among American presidents (perhaps because Elan understates the damage done by Obamacare), Reagan did "instigate the Iran-Contra affair," "let federal spending rise," "did not reduce big government," and cancelled out the benefits of a large tax cut by not coupling it with spending cuts.

The lesson here is plain. When you get down to the brass tacks of which American presidents most embodied the values of peace, prosperity, and liberty (PP & L), you find only few—a handful really—acted wisely, avoided unnecessary wars, "demonstrated restrain in economic crisis" and foreign affairs, practiced free-market capitalism and favored hard money; opposed big government and welfare, and limited executive and federal power.

Ranked Number One is the stellar John Tyler. He ended "the worst Indian wars in U.S. history," practiced restraint in an international dispute, "opposed big government and protected states' powers." Grover Cleveland is second, as an "exemplar of honesty and limited government." Martin van Buren excelled—especially in rejecting economic stimulus and national debt and balancing budgets. He ranks third. Rutherford B. Hayes is fourth. Likewise, he didn't just preach but practiced capitalism and advocated for black voting rights, while recognizing the ruthlessness of Reconstruction.

In the context of the American presidency and our lost Constitution, Beck's alarm over candidate Trump is peculiar. Not many American presidents lived up to republican ideas of liberty and limited authority.

"Where are the people who say we stand with the Constitution," protested Beck. Trump fails to talk about the Constitution in depth, he blathered.

True. Trump is not a TV talker. Moreover, all candidates who talk about the Constitution "in depth" are dishonest. *For there is no Constitution left to talk about.* That thing died over the course of centuries of legislative, executive and judicial usurpation. That's why when Iraqis were composing their Constitution (after Number 43 destroyed their country), the late Joe Sobran recommended we give them ours because we don't use it.

Mention of the Constitution means nothing. It's on the list of items candidates check when they con constituents. Beck went on to OMG it about Trump saying this:

"President Obama's irresponsible use of executive orders has paved the way for him to also use them freely if he wins the presidential race."

Amen—provided Trump uses executive power to *repeal* lots of laws, not *make* them. We live under an administrative "Secret State." Very many, maybe most, of the laws under which Americans labor ought to be repealed. The only laws that are naturally inviolable are those upholding life, liberty and property.

Trump, thankfully, has proclaimed: "The one thing good about executive orders [is that] the new president, if he comes in – boom, first day, first hour, first minute, you can rescind that."

Beck has protested. He apparently accepts the inherent legitimacy of Barack Obama's executive orders. Beck also seems to believe that the Constitution, or some other higher order, demands that people continue to labor under burdensome government edicts forever after, and that to promise repeal is the act of a progressive.

"Ted Cruz," countered Beck, who has since endorsed candidate Cruz, "is the guy who says he's for certain principles and will be tethered and tied to them, exactly like Ronald Reagan was."

Well, another of Eland's discomforting observations about Reagan is that he "enhanced executive power through questionable means. Although presidential signing statements, accompanying bills passed by Congress, had been around since George Washington, Reagan began to use these signing statements to contravene or nullify Congress's will without giving that body a chance to override a formal presidential veto."

There's nothing necessarily progressive about overturning laws that have been passed.

There is nothing sacred about every law an overweening national government and its unelected agencies impose on the people. "At the federal level alone," the number of laws totaled 160,000 pages," in 2012. By broadcaster John Stossel's estimation, "Government adds 80,000 pages of rules and regulations every year." According to the *Heritage Foundation*, "Congress continues to criminalize at an average rate of one new crime for every week of every year."

America has become a nation of thousands-upon-thousands of arbitrary laws, whose effect is to criminalize naturally licit conduct.

Is Beck implying, in his objection to Trump's promise to repeal Obama's executive orders, that laws subjecting over 300 million people to the edicts of one have moral force?

Rather than uphold individual rights, most positive law regulates or criminalizes the business of life.

On February 13, well before going to press with this volume, conservative Justin Antonin Scalia, sitting on the Supreme Court of the United States, shuffled this mortal coil. Justice Scalia had been dead a few hours, when President Barack Obama put Senator Mitch McConnell and his patsy Republicans on notice as to their obligation to fill the vacancy. For his part, the president threatened to exercise his constitutional authority by foisting on the country another rogue in robes: Obama has appointed progressive activists Sonia Sotomayor and Elena Kagan to the SCOTUS. Before him, George Bush had given us John Roberts who begot the coercive ObamaCare.

Any forestalling in the speedy appointment of a Scalia replacement, the president, and Democrats Hillary Clinton and Harry Reid hurried to frame as a thwarting of the American people's democratic rights.

Nonsense on stilts.

In its guide to the Constitution's Appointments Clause, the Heritage Foundation explains that, "Both the debates among the Framers and subsequent practice confirm that the President has [exclusive] plenary power to nominate" principal officers. Through its representatives, the public reserves the power of confirmation. The Senate thus "possesses the plenary authority to reject or confirm the nominee"; it has "complete and final discretion in whether to accept or approve a nomination." Alas, "its weaker structural position means that [the Senate] is likely to confirm most nominees, absent compelling reasons to reject them."

Indeed, the libertarian contention that liberty is not necessarily safeguarded by the Constitution was bolstered by Virginian George Mason, "a delegate to the U.S. Constitutional Convention of 1787." The President has an unfair advantage:

> When the President has a substantial basis of party support in the Senate and thus a nucleus of probable supporters, he has leverage for

confirmation. Thus, the image of a divided government as a government in any sense equally divided when it comes to an analysis of the Appointments Clause and the confirmation process is a fundamentally false image. (*The Heritage Guide to the Constitution's Appointments Clause.*)

Senator Chuck Schumer vowed in 2007 to oppose the confirmation of a Supreme Court judge during George Bush's lame duck session, the time "between election day and the day that new legislators and president assume office." Now the Democrat from New York is excoriating Republicans as obstructionists for expressing the same sentiment, namely that the next president should be the one to "replace deceased Supreme Court Justice Antonin Scalia."

To repeat the theme that threads this volume, *we're down to action and counteraction, force and counterforce in the service of liberty.*

Above all, Article II, Section 2, Clause 2 of the US Constitution is procedural law written by men; it is not natural law.

Ultimately, nobody in the U.S., not even government, may kill and enslave somebody or rob them of property without due process. The procedural delay in legislation that does not impinge on these individual rights to life, liberty and private property is nothing to fuss about. Republicans may delay the appointment of a Scalia replacement till the cows come home without violating the individual rights of a single American.

Failing to legislate or nullifying man-made laws comports with American freedoms just fine. Donald Trump had better sit at his desk for a chunk of his first term and issue one executive order after the other to do just that.

~January 22, 2016

16. THE ME-MYSELF-AND-I MEGYN PRODUCTION MESSES WITH TRUMP

The Iowa caucuses are upon us. Every sentient human being who has lived through the Trump revolution thinks Donald J. Trump, the *enfant terrible* of establishment politics, will likely win the Republican caucuses, come February 1.

As of January 27, an Iowa Monmouth University Poll places Trump at thirty percent to Texas Senator Ted Cruz's twenty-three percent, up from nineteen percent last month. At forty-one percent nationwide, Trump's lead is double that of Cruz, his closest rival.

Other than news emanating from the Me-Me Megyn Kelly megaphone—most media predict a "huge" turnout among Republican caucus-goers, enthusiasm that's hard to associate with Ted's pompous, preachy sermons. ("Inauthenticity" is how Rand Paul put it.)

Still, not all media have learned to refrain from projecting their innermost desires onto and into their reporting. So when The Donald upset the political applecart again, January 26, some still posed numbingly stupid questions that ignore the candidate's trajectory:

"Will Trump's big debate gamble be brilliant or disastrous for his campaign?"

"Will Trump's Boycott Play as Tantrum or Principled?"

The Me-Myself-I Megyn Production Messes With Trump

The special-needs media's professional retardation is a source of lots of laughter on Twitter:

CNN's Ryan Lizza, "Trump is basically winning a multi-front war against every power center of the Republican Party."

MSNBC's Joe Scarborough: "Anyone thinking Trump loses this game of chicken hasn't been paying attention for the past six months."

"Trump just shot Fox News in the middle of Fifth Avenue," tweeted another, alluding to Trump bragging he "could stand in the middle of 5th Avenue and shoot somebody and [he] wouldn't lose any voters."

And: "So it turns out Fox WILL be hosting an undercard debate."

Here's what just happened: Donald Trump had not expected to be subjected again to Megyn Kelly's ministrations, after the anchor's missteps during the first prime-time Republican debate, in Cleveland, Ohio, last year.

The consensus among very many outside the Beltway bubble was that the smug Megyn Kelly had been rude and overbearing during that debate, clobbering Trump with sub-intelligent, war-on-women questions.

Donald Trump had implicitly, at least, expected the network to rethink its decision to unleash showy Ms. Kelly, once again, on the occasion of a Republican debate, scheduled for January 28.

It's hard to believe Kelly's higher-ups at FNC are so stupid as to put her in the moderator's chair again. Given the woman's profile, I suspect Fox's Golden Goose had henpecked the boss, Roger Ailes, to have at it again.

Kelly's central focus is to be center-stage. This her unbecoming conduct over months has made clear. *The Kelly File*, Megyn's show, has persistently ignored news about the news-maker of the day, Donald Trump. Yet just this once, Kelly elected to extensively cover Trump's decision not to attend a debate moderated by herself, to whom she referred adoringly as "yours truly."

"Yours truly" was the theme of the January 26 segment.

And the guests stampeded to her studio for a chance to genuflect to Kelly and diss the front-runner for the umpteenth time. This time it would be different. This time, Trump was going down.

Kelly's "Breaking News" coverage entailed parading other candidates past and present to berate Trump's actions—to call him a coward, running scared of a woman; to question the candidate's commitment to Iowans, label him someone who doesn't show-up, when Trump has been in Iowa all along, showing Iowans The Love.

Especially asinine was the snarky Millennial-like press release Fox News chose to put out in response—a release that cemented Donald Trump's decision to do something more useful and foil the Megyn Kelly extravaganza.

The notice was too frivolous for actor Sean Penn to have penned (we recently discovered Penn could write). Perhaps the ghost writer was goofy, late-night show host Jimmy Fallon?

> We learned from a secret back channel that the
> Ayatollah and Putin both intend to treat Donald
> Trump unfairly when they meet with him if he
> becomes president — a nefarious source tells us
> that Trump has his own secret plan to replace
> the Cabinet with his Twitter followers to see if
> he should even go to those meetings ...

Come again?

Actually, the network's juvenile jab at Trump sounds remarkably like ... Megyn Kelly. In an attempt to shape news, not report it, Kelly has reported minimally on the newsmaker-in-chief. But the anchor has been consistently snarky in her sparing "coverage" of Trump, over the months.

Nasty nightly are Kelly's sidekicks, Chris Stirewalt and Howard Kurtz ("Howie," as Kelly calls him). Together, the three berate Trump and his *lumpenproletariat*, including any media that cover him. Kelly has crowed about "rerun" interviews; and congratulated herself on air for not being "all Trump, all the time," when she, in fact, covers Trump hardly at all.

But you'd have to see the Kelly cobra in action to appreciate the venom with which the following words were spat out:

"Many more men like Donald Trump than women. Hispanics and African-American are not crazy about Donald Trump." His base consists of whites without college degrees.

"He's very smart at manipulating some media." (Here Kelly pulls a face to distinguish herself from the pack).

"Fact checking Donald Trump is like picking up after a dog with diarrhea." (A favorite *Kelly File* guest gets guffaws.)

"Is the front-runner on the GOP side an honest person?" (That's Kelly floating suggestive *ad hominem*.)

So, is Kelly a consummate professional or is she a consummate self-promoter, preoccupied with the production that is Megyn Kelly? Differently put, how professional is Kelly?

Not very.

It matters not who was right or wrong during the first round—did Trump object *illegitimately* to the so-called piercing arrows in Kelly's intellectual quiver? Or was the candidate *legitimately* offended by the anchor's foolish identity politics on display?

A serious journalist with a grasp of the enormity of the Trump revolution; a journalist who didn't wish to give up on ever again interviewing the candidate, or forever forfeit access to a possible future president; a journalist with gravitas would have labored less at promoting herself and more on mending a professional relationship.

Not Kelly. And Kelly's colleagues and bosses are enablers; they've taught her everything about ratings, make-up and hair. (Yes, your new hair is magnificent, Megyn Kelly. Glad you got rid of the old, matted shag that likely needed extensive reviving before each show. You're a pretty girl. But boy, are you vain and a tad vacuous. The way you always bring the *Kelly File* show back to ... yourself. Does that take skill or just all-consuming narcissism?) Alas, not much have her mentors taught Kelly about off-camera, unglamorous, shoe-leather journalism.

Namely, you are not the story. Your job is to get the story.

So what did our lady so fair do over the holidays to fix her professional *faux pa*? Kelly took her sassy keister to *Vanity Fair*, where her pictures were splayed over the glossy magazine's pages. Trump, she told the You-Go-Girl journalists at VF, had attempted to woo Ms. everybody-wants-me Kelly. Now what do you think about that!

Suppose Trump had tried to curry favor with Kelly. Is that something a professional who still wishes to interact with her subject shares publicly? No! Kelly's actions all along have been those of a woman who sees herself as a personality first. As an ego in an anchor's chair, or a woman scorned, Kelly is game to go up against Trump.

As I noted, *The Kelly File* has kept up a barrage of hostilities against Trump, since the August fall-out. The man has a case against Kelly.

For a time following the much-needed dressing-down and time-out forced by her snarling attack on Trump, last year, Kelly was slightly more serious, more demure. She has since rebounded with a vengeance. After Vanity Fair, off our fair lady rushed to make hay on the *Charlie Rose Show*, where she was utterly charming, as she indubitably is. Until you stop to analyze her actions.

The onslaught of Kelly charisma has become tiresome and off-putting.

With Charlie Rose, Kelly, as always, brought it back to herself: She told the interviewer how Fox News boss Roger Aisles had liked "the package: the smarts, the looks, the voice." Her words about herself.

During the Rose interview, we learned from motormouth that because she's so cute (presumably), she was given a stripper name by her sources when investigating a story about a stripper who cried rape.

When she first burst on to the Fox News scene, years ago, Kelly announced in an interview that she was beautiful inside and out. She left out boastful.

As to Fox and friends' brave stand for *their* freedom of press and *against* Trump's freedom of association: Contrary to Geraldo Rivera's confused assertion, Donald Trump had not dictated to Fox News, but dissociated from the network this once.

"Lol [laughing out loud], Donald J. Trump isn't scared, he's efficient with his time," tweeted Alec. Trump will be holding a competing (fundraising) event in Iowa. If the competition to Fox News takes it upon itself to send in the cameramen—Trump's event will probably trump the specter of "two Cubans arguing," in ratings (as another tweet taunted).

Fox News has since compounded its problems by using "terrorizing" to describe the Trump campaign's "vicious attacks" on Kelly. That's underhanded.

"When the ladies operate within a protective penumbra of political correctness in a highly feminized culture of girly men, it is pretty easy to win intellectual pillow fights," wrote Kent G. Bailey, Ph.D., professor emeritus of clinical psychology at Virginia Commonwealth University.

Basking in the glow of low T candidates, once again, Megyn Kelly's girly gutter journalism was on display at the debate in Des Moines, Iowa, January 28.

"Let's address the elephant not in the room tonight," she taunted, pausing to bat eyelashes Bambi-like. "Senator Cruz, what message do you think Trump's absence sends to the voters of Iowa?"

Let me answer Kelly with logic, not with feminine wiles. Kelly's question is a leading question, not a probative question, because the question suggests the answer. Hers is a bad-faith question.

The Left is going to love Megyn Kelly even more for supposedly intimidating Donald Trump. For Kelly to love herself more is impossible.

~January 29, 2016

17. THE WINNING TRUMP TICKET AND CABINET

If Donald J. Trump wishes to lessen the impact of his disappointing second in the Iowa caucuses and walk back the tack he's taken with Ted Cruz—he must begin to think big and talk big.

Loud in not necessarily big.

Call it triangulation, a concept associated with Bill Clinton's successful strategies, or call it "the art of the deal": It's time for Trump to DO IT.

To this end, Trump must quit the "we don't win anymore" formulaic rhapsody, and start fleshing out substantive positions. A pragmatist does so by introducing the people he'll be recruiting to "Make America Great Again."

To Cruz belongs the Trump Department of Justice portfolio. Offering Justice to Cruz allows Trump to both put Ted in his place as unsuited to the presidency; while simultaneously making him part of Team Trump and repairing that relationship.

Ted is too soft to be U.S. president in these troubled times. But he'd make a spectacular attorney general in charge of DOJ.

There's a reason George W. Bush hates Ted Cruz. In 2008, Cruz gave America reason to cue the mariachi band and celebrate the death of detritus José Medellín.

As part of a gangbanger initiation rite, Medellín had raped (in every way possible), strangled, slashed, and stomped two young Texan girls to death.

"In Texas," to quote another Ron from the Lone Star State, "we have the death penalty and we use it. If you come to Texas and kill somebody, we will kill you back." (I give you comedian Ron White.)

Bush 43 would wrestle a crocodile for a criminal alien. Backed by Bush—and on behalf of Medellín and other killer compadres awaiting a similar fate—Mexico promptly sued the U.S. over petty procedural technicalities in the International Court of Justice. The president ordered Texas to halt the execution of murderer and rapist Medellín.

Texas' heroic solicitor general said no.

Cruz took the case to the Supreme Court. There, he bested Bush and his lickspittles. As the Conservative Review gloated, Cruz "won the case, six-to-three." He had sought justice for Americans against a president who subjugated them to international courts. Ted, moreover, was forever gracious about Bush; Bush and his *bambino* bro routinely slime Ted.

In trashing Texas Senator Ted Cruz, Trump is in bad company.

The American government currently outsources the job of vetting Muslim refugees headed for the US to the most corrupt of UN agencies: the United Nations High Commissioner for Refugees.

If anyone can vanquish the UN and extricate America from sovereignty sundering international treaties—it's the victor in Medellín v. Ted of Texas.

Next is Rand Paul. The senator has abandoned hopes of becoming president of the United States, in 2016. With his departure, the libertarian bloom is off the Republican race for the White House.

Rand has been the only Republican in the running to sound a strong trumpet against the warfare state of his rivals. If a giant welfare state is unconservative, what of the warfare state?

By logical extension, not signing on to the bombing of Bashar Hafez al-Assad was a good thing, observed Rand. Assad was the source of stability in Syria, much as Saddam Hussein was in Iraq. Have we learned nothing about the perils of toppling dictators, only to see the rise of barbarians worse than their predecessors?

Besides, why are we still at war in Afghanistan? Why are we dropping bombs there? Why have we been "helping" Afghanistan for over ten years, inquired Rand in the course of his campaign? We've spent more in that blighted and benighted region than we did on the Marshall Plan. "Why can't the Afghans defend themselves after a decade? Will we have to defend them in perpetuity?"

And what's unconservative about diplomatic engagement?

As impure a libertarian as he is, when compared to father Ron Paul, Rand has mocked his rivals' military chauvinism and jingoism as incompatible with conservatism.

In particular, why was the robotic Marco Rubio being given the time of day? Rubio is spoiling for fights that'll dwarf the wars Barack Obama and Hillary Clinton waged on Libya, surreptitiously in Syria and in Afghanistan. As president, "the Boy in the Bubble" (Governor Chris Christie's moniker for Marco) has promised to use American power extremely liberally. Or, as Rand has kept reminding Americans, there is no daylight between the Rubio and Hillary Clinton regime-change foreign policy.

Rand has been rather rude to Donald Trump, who, in turn, has not spared Senator Paul his repartee. But the front-runner, not Rand, has some placating to do.

Promise Rand Paul a cabinet position as secretary of state in charge of U.S. foreign policy. Trump will thus bring the libertarians in from the cold. (By Gallop's count, the libertarian-leaning vote might be as large as twenty-four percent.)

Rand can have State on one condition.

In the past, Trump has praised Representative Ron Paul. Trump will further solidify libertarian backing if he places Paul senior in charge of the U.S. Department of the Treasury. Independents and some on the Left may follow (although they'll lie to pollsters about it). No one is better suited than Congressman Paul to the task of halting further debasement of the coin courtesy of the Federal Reserve Bank. He will also put an end to the depravity that is the Internal Revenue Service.

The urgency of the strategy offered in this column dawned when a ghastly idea was floated on Twitter to approving "Retweets": "Trump should choose Colin Powell as VP." Powell was the establishment toady who endorsed the war on Iraq while in the employ of Genghis Bush. Later, General Powell backed Barack Obama, using the pathos of racial justice as his excuse. In Trump parlance, Powell would be a "horrible" mistake. The same can be said about Ann Coulter's calamitous Trump-Mitt Romney suggested ticket.

No, *Trump must go outside the political tribe for a vice president.*

A previous chapter in this volume suggested "the talented James Webb" for the Trump ticket. Webb is a decorated Marine who served as Ronald Reagan's secretary of the navy. In particular, Webb is the recipient of the "Navy Cross for heroism in Vietnam," the Silver Star, two Bronze Stars, and two Purple Hearts.

Indisputably the last salt-of-the-earth Democrat of his generation, Webb had considered a bid for president as a Democrat, last year. However, he appeared out of place at the first dominatrix-dominated debate in October of 2015, where he confessed to killing a man or two in battle. He soon dropped out.

Citing paleoconservative thinker Pat Buchanan, Mr. Webb had argued forcefully against affirmative action and for poor whites, well before reports about the early demise of white working-class percolated to the public.

Webb the Southern Democrat can galvanize Reagan Democrats as well as fans of the military on the Left.

Rand Paul will bring libertarians along provided the little guy brings his dad to work with him.

Wasted on the presidency is an outstanding mind like that of Senator Ted Cruz. An outstanding businessman like Donald Trump should appreciate the intellectual value of such an asset.

~February 5, 2016

18. THE MURDOCH MEDIA: ROOT 'N BRANCH FOR MARCOBOT

"Wish-fulfillment is "the satisfaction of a desire through an involuntary thought process." This Freudian term encapsulates the coverage of the riveting 2016 primaries by the Megyn Kelly wing (or coven) of the Murdoch Media.

Yes, a news personality—a showgirl really—is running more of Roger Ailes' show than she should. And, as Newsmax reports, not everyone in the Fox News org is pleased with Kelly's "Trump-fueled stardom."

Since the anchoring philosopher in Kelly's life is Oprah Winfry's protégé TV pop-psychologist Dr. Phil—the anchor ought to appreciate a psychological idiom that encapsulates her coverage of the New Hampshire primary, in particular, and of Donald Trump in general.

Look, no-one is discounting the news-worthy value of good leg and hair action and some, but not much, fine *couture*. However, *Kelly File* coverage is defined by little to no analysis approximating reality, hence "wish fulfillment."

What the likes of lightweight Dana Perino, Mega-ego Kelly and their male friendlies have made manifest is that: 1) Navigating the shoals of reality is hard for them, and 2) They're hoping against hope that someone will politically slay The Donald dragon.

The central question around which these Marco-Rubio enamored performers have thus framed the New Hampshire primary's results is: Who is going to beat Mr. Trump, the Republican front runner, who'd just triumphed "big league" in NH.

The headline on kingmaker Kelly's Fox News website was, "What's the anti-Trump strategy now?" (It has since vanished.) And, "Who will the lead GOP establishment?" On February 10, Kelly scolded Jeb Bush for "having his eye on the wrong guy," and failing to take on the "quarterback who's running with the ball."

To the extent *The Kelly File* covers the Trump phenomenon, coverage is given over to plotting against the candidate and, by extension, the Americans he represents.

The desire among select members of the Murdoch Media for a Marco Rubio victory is in plain view. Kelly and her carefully selected compadres are hoping against hope that Trump will stop winning. Their focus, to the exclusion of all else, is on who'll stop their political *bête noire*.

News coverage that is directed toward desired outcomes is no coverage at all.

Surprisingly, MSNBC's coverage of the NH primaries was way more analytical. Instead of practicing Freudian "wish fulfillment," and ruminating about the ways in which their preferred candidate could beat his rotten rival— MSNBC anchors "analyzed": They pointed out that, "Both parties' winners in NH signal changes for the U.S.," and that the "Trump win could transform American politics."

Almost correct. It's not Trump that's transforming American politics; it's the people of America doing the transforming. Trump is merely channeling the "noisy-as-hell majority."

MSNBC commentator Rachel Maddow nearly got it right when she suggested that "Donald Trump's win in New Hampshire could represent a shift in American politics and the Republican Party to compare more closely with right-wing nativist political parties in Europe." Were I Ms. Maddow's Roger Ailes, however, I'd have asked her to scrub news coverage of the pejoratives "xenophobic" and "nativist." Reserve those for her own opinion-driven show, if she must.

Why, the left-liberal Ms. Maddow might serve as a professional role model for Megyn Kelly, whose métier is feel-good militarism, anti-Trumpism and you-go-girl, hybrid feminism.

Again, at least MSNBC anchors "analyzed"; including to hark back to the populist uprising led by Pat Buchanan, who won the New Hampshire 1992 Republican presidential primaries.

Fresh from a sledding contest in NH with other sexy (but not very smart) co-hosts like herself, unsharpened pencil Perino ventured, on Fox News, that the Marcobot's malfunction was a once-off glitch, nothing major.

Needless to say, if you joined the Foxettes, as too many of you did—to judge from their winning ratings—you'd struggle to decipher the hushed references to Senator Rubio's so-called single mishap.

And, if you missed the February 6 debate and have since been relying on Fox for news, you'd be clueless about the incident, which—bar Megyn Kelly's absence from center stage—was one of the highlights of the ABC Republican debate in New Hampshire.

The meltdown saw Marcobot repeat the following paragraph several times:

> Let's dispel with this fiction that Barack Obama doesn't know what he's doing. He knows exactly what he's doing. He is trying to change this country. He wants America to become more like the rest of the world. We don't want to be like the rest of the world, we want to be the United States of America. And when I'm elected president, this will become once again, the single greatest nation in the history of the world, not the disaster Barack Obama has imposed upon us.

An eerie encounter with Robo-Rubio had been documented as far back as December 23, last year. Again, if you rely on Fox News for election coverage, you'd be unaware of the impressions imparted by a New Hampshire newspaper.

Observed *The Conway Daily Sun*:

> Watching [Rubio] was like witnessing a computer algorithm designed to cover talking points. He said a lot, but at the same time said nothing. It was like someone wound him up, pointed him towards the doors, and pressed

play. If there was a human side, a soul, to the senator, it did not come through.

Ignored, too, was a pre-debate, anti-Marco Rubio ad run by Governor Chris Christie. The ad captured another memorized, unresponsive line repeated *ad nauseam* by Rubio, in all interviews:

"The presidency of the United States is a unique office, it's not like being a senator but it's not like being a governor, either." (Two minutes and fifty three seconds into the clip titled "Root of Rubio gaffe: confirming suspicions he's scripted.")

In fairness to Marco Rubio, at least he remembers his rehearsed lines; Barack Obama needs a teleprompter to remind him of his.

It's proving very hard to reboot Rubio.

A day after Marco's debate night malfunction, the senator went straight back to "explaining his canned talking points with ... more canned talking points":

"I'm going to continue saying that, because it's at the core of our campaign."

"I'm going to continue saying that, because it's one of the reasons I'm running."

"I'm going to continue saying that, because not only is it the truth, it's at the core of our campaign."

"At the core of this campaign is that statement, and I'm going to continue to say it."

There's more of the same but columnists are bound by a word count.

A gaffe, an odd moment, a bad night is how the Marcobot Media has framed Rubio's recitations. (At least three of the country's smartest female columnists have been warning about Rubio for years. The one is Ann Coulter; the other Phyllis Schlafly. Modesty prevents this column from naming the third, but she has been pairing Rubio and the adjectives "robotic" and "neoconservative" for some time.)

Governor Christie has taken himself out of the presidential race. He is, nevertheless, owed a debt of gratitude for exposing Rubio's faulty circuitry.

Inadvertently has Christie done the country another kindness: He has given viewers a glimpse into the low-watt, spiteful coverage coming from the Kelly arm of the Murdoch Media.

~February 12, 2016

19. MAKING AMERICA GREAT MEANS TAKING DOWN 'W'

Making America great again, the theme of Donald Trump's 2016 campaign, depends on dispelling the myths and myth-making that made America bad.

Beginning with George W. Bush.

Said Saint Augustine: "The confession of evil works is the first beginning of good works."

The Republican Party under Bush did the devil's work. Bar the sainted Ron Paul, not a dog of a Republican lifted his leg in protest of the unjust war on Iraq.

To embark on the good, the GOP must come clean about the bad. To that end, Donald Trump has begun a vital process of expiation.

The 43rd president is categorized as "bad" and ranked 37th by Ivan Eland, previously mentioned, author of *Recarving Rushmore: Ranking the Presidents on Peace, Prosperity, and Liberty*. Having undermined the republic at home and peace abroad, "Bush's presidency," avers Eland, "was one of the worst of all time."

Coming to terms with the Bush legacy, moreover, ought to prevent the rise of another Bush. For the bogus Bush Doctrine is alive and well-exploited in the words and promises of each of the Republican candidates, bar Donald Trump.

Making America Great Means Taking Down 'W'

The Bush dictum of fighting them over *there* so they don't come *here*—as if Islamic State can't, won't and hasn't attacked *there* and *here*—is alive and well-exploited by almost every fork-tongued politician in the Republican and Democratic races.

Other than Trump and Bernie Sanders, there's a potatoes vs. spuds quality to the foreign policy articulated by both sides.

Each time the interchangeable John Kasich or Marco Rubio or Jeb Bush are asked about death by Muslim *in* the United States; they whip out that dumb "W" Doctrine, tethering attacks like San Bernardino *in* the U.S. to wars the U.S. *should* be waging over in the Middle East, and *will be* waging if these candidates have their way.

If you liked Bush's willful, criminal war on Iraq; if you enjoyed watching aw-shucks "W" "Shock and Awe" Iraq to kingdom come with BLU-82s—boy, do you have a treat in store.

If you took pleasure in Bush unseating and executing law-and-order leader Saddam Hussein; you'll love the plans Rubio, Kasich and Brother Jeb have for Bashar Assad and his family. As for Vladimir Putin, the not-so-comical three stooges have practically diarized conflagration with Russia.

I almost forgot: If you licked your chops when Bush disarmed dem little Iraqi boys by littering their playgrounds with cluster bomblets; your vampiric urges will be sated. In Bush's Baghdad, hospitals teamed with limbless kids successfully disarmed. The Rubio-Kasich-Bush bandidos will similarly oblige their supporters. Happy times are ahead for their acolytes.

In brother Jeb, promised George Bush in South Carolina, on February 16, the country will be getting a "steady hand" to steer the ship of state.

Yes, in his many addresses to the nation, during the crises into which he plunged America, Bush used to bang on about the joys of bringing about "the triumph of democracy and tolerance in Iraq, in Afghanistan and beyond."

Plenty of that poppycock awaits America should Bush III or his other three foreign-policy clones materialize in the White House. Hawk Hillary must be added to present company, as nation building at the point of a bayonet makes her barking happy. (The rabid Mrs. Clinton has taken to barking at her campaign rallies. Check it out on YouTube.)

Laudably and mercilessly did Trump taunt Jeb Bush at the CBS News Republican debate, in South Carolina, February 13. Jeb had brought out Big Brother to fight his battles for him:

Said Trump: "The war in Iraq was a big, fat mistake. All right? Now, you can take it any way you want ... George Bush made a mistake. We can make mistakes. But that one was a beauty. We should have never been in Iraq. We have destabilized the Middle East."

Why would the guy, Donald J. Trump, take up Rand Paul's libertarian foreign policy stance when he leads among Republican voters? So asked a Republican strategist on *Hardball*, Chris Matthews' MSNBC show.

The special-needs media was abuzz, questioning Trump's anti-G. Bush "tactics."

But badmouthing G. Bush to a South Carolina electorate, apparently still partial to the man, is no tactic; it's a higher calling. The reason Trump has no qualms about repudiating Bush II's colossal war crime—the invasion of Iraq—is because he speaks the truth.

Trump is not a politician. To hear Ted Cruz tell it, Trump's past support of this or the other position was done in a political capacity. Cruz forgets that Trump was a civilian.

And unlike Hillary Clinton and every single Republican and their media mouths—Trump is not ankle deep in the blood of hundreds of thousands of Iraqis and other Middle-Easterners, Muslim and Christian. He didn't cast a deciding vote to prosecute their war and he had the good sense to question it in his limited capacity as a civilian.

That Trump is accused of sounding like the ladies of Code Pink isn't an argument; it's an *ad hominem* attack. For it is quite possible, even likely, that Code Pink, a restraining influence on jingoism and imperialism, is correct about Bush.

So white-hot is the hate for Donald Trump; that it has united The Machine in defense of the indefensible, George W. Bush

This, too, is understandable considering Mr. Trump's accomplishments:

So far, Trump has upended the Media Complex, the Republican Party Complex (in the form of the Republican

National Committee), and the phony Conservatism Complex. It's time for the War Party faction within to wither, too.

~February 19, 2016

20. TRUMP CALLED BUSH A LIAR & WON SOUTH CAROLINA (NEVADA, TOO)

Donald Trump has buried George W. Bush, for good. Or so we hope. This might not be "Morning in America," but it is a moral victory for values in America. Somewhere in those Judeo-Christian values touted by "values voters" is an injunction against mass murder.

Before the February 20 South Carolina primary, it looked as though G. Bush might just make a comeback.

After the South Carolina primary, where Donald Trump won with 32.2 percent of the Republican vote, it seems certain that nothing will resuscitate the legacy of "one of the nation's worst presidents."

Notwithstanding his war crimes and unprecedented intervention in the financial system and the private economy, "W" also happened to preside over the largest domestic spending since Lyndon Johnson. As chronicled in the most libertarian source on American presidents, Ivan Eland's *Recarving Rushmore: Ranking the Presidents on Peace, Prosperity, and Liberty*, "[Bush] advocated bad policies and demonstrated horrendous operational incompetence."

> The disastrous and expensive (in casualties and money) nation-building project in Iraq and Afghanistan were only exceeded in catastrophic

results by Bush's expansion of executive power and theft of the civil liberties that make the United States unique. Bush had almost no accomplishments to offset such foibles.

Trump addressed the war: "They lied. They said there were weapons of mass destruction. There were none. And they knew there were none. There were no weapons of mass destruction."

The chattering class, Left and Right, was—still is—gobsmacked. A political Samson was bringing down the pillars of their world.

Desperate to restore equilibrium before the crucial SC vote was CNN's Anderson Cooper: "You would not say again that George W. Bush lied?"

Trump obliged. He backpedaled before the primary, going with non-committal: "I don't know. I can't tell you. I mean, I'd have to look at documents."

So America has some unfinished business. Because we do know. We can say for sure. And we have all the documents. George W. Bush lied America into war.

Bush began his ballyhooed presidency by lying during his campaign. He promised America a humble foreign policy, but came into office with the express purpose of using his plenary powers to unseat Saddam Hussein. Reliable sources—vaunted officials such as the former head of the CIA's counterterrorism office, Vincent Cannistraro—attested that Bush started plotting to "settle" old scores with Saddam Hussein as soon as he got to the White House.

Trump Called Bush A Liar & Won South Carolina (Nevada Too)

This was well after the International Atomic Energy Agency (IAEA) vouched Iraq had "dismantled its nuclear program." To good effect, Bush and his bandits dusted off "decade old" IAEA reports and presented these as the *casus belli* for a new war. Yes, the Bush reports about Iraqi Weapons of Mass Destruction (WMD) were a "decade old"; out-of-date and inapplicable, when they were deployed to go to war, in 2003.

In 2004, U.S. weapons inspector David Kay was tasked with a post-invasion investigation as to why no WMD were found in Iraq. The evidence Kay marshaled was the same old evidence those of us who opposed the war cited back in the dying days of 2002. Having publicly fumed about the impotence of the IAEA's much-maligned inspection process, Kay found himself in the embarrassing position of vouching for IAEA effectiveness.

IAEA inspectors were, in fact, still crisscrossing Iraq when Bush invaded.

For his 2004 tome *Plan of Attack*, author Bob Woodward was given his usual unparalleled access. Woodward conducted 75-odd interviews with members of the Bush administration's inner sanctums, Bush too. Woodward concluded, and was lauded by the proud culprits themselves: "Bush is in charge. Bush is all over [Iraq]."

"Just five days after September 11," by Woodward's telling, "the president indicated to National Security Adviser Condoleezza Rice that he was determined to do something about Saddam Hussein."

On November 21, 2001, the bombastic Bush, who had characterized his war as "the story of the 21st Century," demanded an invasion plan from Secretary of Defense Donald Rumsfeld.

"Get on it," Bush barked.

General Tommy Franks was then given *carte blanche* to develop such a strategy, for which the president, unbeknownst to Congress, siphoned $700 million from a supplemental appropriation for the Afghan War.

On February 16, 2002, Bush signed a "Top Secret intelligence order" granting authority to the CIA and the military to commence covert operations in Iraq. December 21, 2002 saw CIA Director George Tenet and his deputy John McLaughlin summoned to the Oval Office to screen a slideshow of Iraq's alleged WMD. The president took the lead. He made it clear that Tenet had to deliver on his promise of an intelligence "slam dunk." Alas, G. Bush was wholly unimpressed by the "rough cut":

"Nice try, but that isn't gonna sell Joe Public."

"Richard Clark, the White House anti-terrorism coordinator, reported that on the day after 9/11, even after he protested that there was no connection between Saddam Hussein and the 9/11 attacks, Bush personally insisted that he look for one." Clark's memo disavowing such a connection was returned by the "office of Bush's National Security Adviser with the comment: 'Wrong answer. Do it again.'"

Soon, Secretary of State Rice was filling her days with forecasts of a Saddam-seeded nuclear-winter. On September

Trump Called Bush A Liar & Won South Carolina (Nevada Too)

8, 2002, this liar told CNN's Wolf Blitzer that, "We do know that there have been shipments into Iraq of aluminum tubes that really are only suited to nuclear weapons programs." David Albright of the Institution for Science and International Security was appalled. "That's just a lie," he reiterated to *New Republic*.

The "Lie Factory—the Office of Special Plans"—was a central edifice of the Bush administration. The OSP, reminisces Justin Raimondo in a retrospective about Bush's lies, was "a parallel intelligence-gathering agency set up by the neoconservatives in the administration [to feed] Congress and the media 'factoids' which were later proven to be false."

To make his sub-intelligent case for war, Bush mustered the fictitious uranium from Africa, the aluminum tubes from Timbuktu, the invisible "meetings" with al-Qaida in Prague, an al-Qaida training camp that existed under Kurdish—not Iraqi—control, as well as the alleged weaponized chemical and biological stockpiles and their attendant delivery systems that inspectors doubted were there and which never-ever materialized.

"Guilt is an intrinsic quality of actions," wrote the 19th-century American philosopher of liberty, Lysander Spooner. Judging by the actions they commanded, former President George Bush and his "neoconservative Rasputins" were—are—as guilty as sin for the crime of Iraq.

Before his February 23 victory in the Nevada caucuses, fresh from the win in South Carolina, Trump returned to Fox News to dance on George Bush's political grave.

Pompous Chris Wallace imagined he'd get the upper hand with Donald Trump, but ended up changing the subject ... quickly.

"The pundits, including yourself," blasted a triumphant Trump, "thought I made a mistake when I took on Bush on that issue. But when I took on Bush on that issue, I never felt it was a bad thing to do because people that are smart know that the war in Iraq was a disaster."

No more "neoconservative Rasputins." "Fool me once, shame on you; fool me twice, shame on me." Or, in Bushspeak: "Fool me once, shame on ... shame on you. Fool me ... You can't get fooled again!"

~February 26, 2016

21. TRUMP NATION SICK 'N TIRED OF RACIAL SADOMASOCHISM

Van Jones was having a tantrum on TV. The former special advisor for green jobs to Barack Obama, and all-round politically privileged and successful African-American, was demanding that Donald Trump, forthwith, get "passionate" about the black community.

Atone The Donald must for allegedly cozying up to the Klan.

The dust-up was about David Duke, former grand wizard of the Ku Klux Klan. Duke had endorsed Trump. Trump was supposed to flagellate for it. He didn't. When CNN's Jake Tapper pressed a peeved Trump to disavow the Duke endorsement; Trump hummed and hawed, and seemed generally annoyed at the reprimand.

Apparently, he's not into racial sadomasochism.

It was like, "You say David Duke is behind me? What do you want me to do about it? Stop hyperventilating, Jake. Breathe into a paper bag or something."

Later, Trump tweeted short and sweet: "I disavow."

The New York-Washington axis of evil—that's you, Mr. Jones—went mal (as in grand mal)."What! No sackcloth? No ashes?"

Trump should have answered the tricky Ku Klux Klan question he was asked by media with passion, fulminated an hysterical Van Jones, also on CNN. For the sake of my kid, frothed Jones, flecks of spittle flying from his mouth. For the sake of the children of America.

The effing kids are the conman's cudgel of choice.

Your kids are your business, Mr. Jones; your passions yours, too. No presidential candidate should be in the business of catering to ethnic or racial passions. It's refreshing how switched-off Trump is from the racial-grievance industry.

If you imagined Republican pundits were less unhinged, you're deluded. "Conservative" succubus S.E. Cupp completed the kitschification of the Donald-Duke debate.

The religion of thought control will do strange things to those who succumb to it. S.E. Idiot began talking in tongues. Conservatives have taken to speaking the postmodern gibberish once associated mostly with the pseudo-intellectual Left. "Trump 'Otherizes' others," prattled this pig-ignorant panelist.

Essentially, Trump was unfazed even indifferent. As he should be. Trump's attitude was, in fact, as it should be: Take your imagined thought crimes and guilt-by-association and shove 'em. I'm not responsible for the philosophical bent of the individuals who endorse me.

Van Jones wanted what he is accustomed to getting. Trump must capitulate, come clean; embrace the received tenet of systemic, white racism. Go on a pilgrimage to Selma, Alabama. March to Montgomery. Give the Jones foundation money.

Or, be more like the Democratic presumptive nominee, Hillary Clinton.

At a recent Harlem neighborhood gathering, Hillary rabbited on about systemic racism in America. Whites needed to recognize their privilege and practice humility, she puled. I bet the unemployed, poor, working-class whites of West Virginia—hungry, thanks to the Hillary-Hussein war on the coal industry—are lapping-up that beauty.

America: Are you ready to elect another white-bashing hater as president? Heeeere's Hillary.

Here's the deal. Trump is threatening to destabilize the pillars of the thing columnist Jack Kerwick has termed the Racial-Industrial-Complex (RIC). A lot is riding on that ass. It's a lucrative industry—but more than that. The RIC dictates the terms of the debate about race.

White Lives Matter Less is one creedal pillar of the structure Trump is undermining by ignoring the "Racial-Industrial-Complex." In particular, that savage black crime and hooliganism directed at whites is said to be a myth, an artifact dreamed up by racist victims. Thus did the *New York Times* conflate a "white genocide" tweet re-tweeted by Mr. Trump with racism.

Values are another cudgel of the conman and woman.

Here again, Republicans trump Democrats in invoking "values" to intimidate Americans into behaving in politically pleasing ways.

"That's not who we are," intone Obama, Hillary and their political mafia when incontestable majorities call on curbing Islamic in-migration—a reasonable, non-aggressive measure—to reduce the probability of murder-by-Muslim, stateside.

The same impetus animates the Republicans.

More so than the Democrats are Republicans in the habit of shaming Americans into silence by telling them how aberrant and out-of-sync they are. Or, "this is not who we are."

"If a person wants to be the nominee of the Republican Party," bellowed little House Speaker Paul Ryan, on Capitol Hill, "there can be no evasion and no games. They must reject any group or cause that is built on bigotry. This party does not prey on people's prejudices."

Contra Ryan, Russell Kirk was a real, old-school conservative (look him up). "Values," said Kirk, "are private and frail."

Values enforced become dogma.

In the classical conservative and libertarian traditions values are private things. They must be left to individuals and to civil society to practice and police. Party and state operatives have police powers with which to enforce their "values." Therefore, never-ever are they to preach about or police The People's values.

A government apparatchik's job is to uphold the law. No more.

What our crypto-leftist conservatives are ramming down our proverbial gullets are dogmas, not values. Trump is congenitally incapable of responding seriously to the daily, liberal, anti-white onslaught.

Trump Nation Sick 'N Tired Of Racial Sadomasochism

Following the Communist "tradition," thought crimes and sins of omission—protesting too little, as Donald has done—must be followed by show trials. That's what the GOP, party of purported freedom lovers, plans for Trump and his supporters. Put Donald in the dock for David Duke.

There's a certain genius to the American People in taking the side of Trump on this matter.

See, the no-longer-silent majority is exhausted. Americans are exhausted from being racially ramrodded. They've had enough of the pigment burden. The noisy-as-hell-majority is sick-and-tired of being falsely accused of infractions it's innocent of.

~March 4, 2016

22. TRUMP AND TRADE

Mitt gives Mormons (whom I love) a bad name. I thought Mormons weren't meant to bad-mouth others. Yet Mitt Romney has had nothing but bad things to say about Donald Trump, who is political *tabula rasa*, and has never passed a law in his life.

Neither has Trump ever caused the death of a single Iraqi kid. But the religiously devout Romney called him evil for defiling the precious memory of someone who had caused many thousands of such deaths: Bush II.

The meme about Mitt Romney is that had he attacked Barack Obama with the vim and vigor he reserved for Trump, he might have made it to president. (Likewise, if only Abe Foxman of the Anti-Defamation League went after Muslims who lob bombs at Jews with the passion he reserves for gentiles who raise their right hand in a pledge of support for Trump. Poor Abe is seeing Nazi faces in the clouds again.)

Romney also claimed Trump would "propose thirty-five percent tariff-like penalties," and "would instigate a trade war that would raise prices for consumers, kill export jobs, and lead entrepreneurs and businesses to flee America."

I don't know that Trump favors protective tariffs, import quotas or export subsidies.

I do know that we don't have free trade.

What goes for "free trade," rather, is trade managed by powerful bureaucracies—national and transnational—

central planners concerned with regulating, not freeing, trade; whose goal it is to harmonize labor, health, and environmental laws throughout the developed world. The undeveloped and developing worlds do as they please.

My understanding is that Trump simply wants to make these agreements and organs work for the American people.

I know, too, who did support "labeling China a currency manipulator," so that he could "put in place, if necessary, tariffs where ... they are taking unfair advantage of our manufacturers."

Mitt Romney in 2012.

When it comes to the glories of an aggregate, negative balance of trade, libertarian post-graduate cleverness deserves to be questioned.

All libertarians (check) understand that voluntary exchanges are by definition advantageous to their participants. Costco, my hair stylist and the GTI dealer—all have products or skills I want. Within this voluntary, mutually beneficial relationship, I give up an item I value less, for something I value more: a fee for the desired product or service. My trading partners, whose valuations are in complementary opposition to mine, reciprocate in kind.

Ceteris paribus (all other things being equal), there's nothing wrong with my running a trade deficit with Costco, my hair stylist or my GTI dealer, as I do—just as long as I pay for my purchases.

However, the data demonstrate that Americans, in general, are not paying for their purchases.

Americans, reports Fortune.com, actually have more debt relative to income earned than Greeks. "Indebted U.S. households carry an average credit card balance of $15,706, according to NerdWallet."

Corporate America, say analysts at Goldman Sachs, is also heavily leveraged.

The Federal government is the definition of debt. The U.S. national debt is over nineteen trillion dollars without federal unfunded liabilities. Those exceed $127 trillion, by Forbes' 2014 estimate. Total public debt as a percent of Gross Domestic Product, announced the Federal Reserve Bank of St. Louis, is 100.5 percent.

Our improvident government's debts, liabilities and unfunded promises exceed the collective net worth of its wastrel citizens.

Given these historic trends, it seems silly to dismiss the yawning gap between U.S. exports and U.S. imports as an insignificant economic indicator.

Because of decades of credit-fueled, consumption-based living, the defining current characteristic of our economy is debt—micro and macro; public and private. Unless one is coming from the pro-debt Keynesian perspective, is this not an economically combustive combination?

Non-stop consumption—enabled by government monetary and regulatory policies—has coincided with a transition from a manufacturing-based economy to a service-based one; and from an export- to an import-oriented economy. For some reason, this reality has excited febrile libertarian imaginations.

Trump And Trade

I recall how animated Virginia Postrel, author of *The Future and Its Enemies*, became at the general shift in the American economy from knowledge-related to retail jobs, even faulting the Bureau of Labor Statistics for not recognizing the rise of spa-related personal services—manicure and massage therapy—for the powerhouse growth industries they are.

Historically, America's annual trade deficit has been rising. Libertarians at CATO promise that "[t]rade deficits do not cost jobs. Rising trade deficits," they say, "correlate with falling unemployment rates. Far from being a drag on economic growth, the U.S. economy has actually grown faster in years in which the trade deficit has been rising than in years in which the deficit has shrunk."

Contra the Keynesians who control the economy—and whose thinking some libertarians appear to be propping up intellectually, in this instance—real wealth is created not by printing paper money and galvanizing the globe's governments to buy this government's bonds, but by the production and consumption of products. An abundance of goods, not money income, is what makes for an increase in wealth. A natural shift must, therefore, take place in the U.S. from an economy founded on consumption and credit to one rooted in savings, investment and production.

The U.S. Bureau of Economic Analysis announced, March 4, that "the goods and services deficit was $45.7 billion in January, up one billion from $44.7 billion in December. Year-over-year, the average goods and services deficit increased $1.6 billion from the three months ending in January 2015."

Moreover, from the fact that America purportedly ran trade surpluses during the Great Depression it does not follow that the nation's current trade deficit is inconsequential as economic indices go. It could just as well mean that the economic fundamentals today are worse than they were during the Great Depression, since this country has never before been as deeply in hock as it currently is.

Far from comprising discrete parts, the economy is ineluctably interconnected. The trade deficit belongs to a nation enmeshed in debt.

Trump the business mogul is motivated by the sense that the nimbus of great power that surrounds the U.S. is dissipating. Fair enough. He must, at the same time, search closer to home for the causes of America's economic anemia and for the burdens of doing business in America.

As for Mitt; he got off lightly. Trump's linguistic infelicities are becoming legion—almost as bad as George W. Bush's. At a loss for words to describe Romney, who respects the Republican voter not at all, Trump let him off with a soft, indecisive "sad."

Let's hope Trump's incoherent, meandering pattern of speech doesn't give way to soft talk.

~March 11, 2016

23. TRUMP DOESN'T NEED TO TALK LIKE A CONSERVATIVE

With his decisive victory on Super Tuesday II (March 15), Trump is already winning for America. We've won a reprieve. There will be no 13th Republican debate. It was cancelled by the candidate. Megyn Kelly can save her new outfit and mink eyelashes for the next liberal shindig she attends.

Despite the best efforts of Scarlet Letter "E" Republicans and conservatives, Trump now has 673 out of the 1237 delegates required, 263 more than runner-up Ted Cruz. The *New York Times*—it lies a little less than Fox News—has conceded that "Rubio's exit leaves Trump with an open path to 1,237 delegates."

Alas, bar the last debate, in Coral Gables, Miami, March 10, the other 11 debates have not showcased the best of Trump.

And it's not that Trump doesn't talk like a conservative. Talking like a conservative is meaningless.

The Marco Mattel Doll mouthed near-perfect conservative bulletin points. Pull a string, and Barbie's beau would disgorge conservative words and phrases from a rotating repertoire. Look the other way, and the Cuban Ken was passing liberal legislation with Chucky Schumer (Dem).

Talking like a conservative doesn't mean a politician will act like a conservative. Come to think of it, Republican presidents who've talked and acted conservatively are as elusive as Big Foot. There hasn't been a sighting in maybe a century. A purist would cite Democrat Grover Cleveland as America's last conservative president. He preached and practiced the maxim that "the people must support the government, but the government must not support the people."

True, too, is that conservatives, younger ones, it seems, have adopted much of the Left's Orwellian, illiberal thinking, thankfully alien to The Donald.

While the Left controls the intellectual means of production—schools (primary, secondary, tertiary), media (pixels and print), foundations, think tanks, publishing prints—the "Respectable Right" is hardly on the outs with the liberal smart set.

Both factions agree about the following:

Endless immigration is a net good, as long as it's legal.

Source of immigration is insignificant, as long as it's legal. At heart, every Afghani, Iraqi or Somali are closeted Jeffersonians.

When it comes to racism, whites have come a long way and have a long way to go, *ad infinitum*.

Michelle Fields: New Conservatives get as exercised as liberals about pursuing legal remedies for hysteria. In such a national emergency as Fields caused, the advice of Humphrey Bogart, playing Rick Blaine in *Casablanca* (channeled by Woody Allen in *Play It Again Sam*), should have been considered: "I never saw a dame yet that didn't understand a good slap in the mouth ..."

Fields, a reporter, claimed she was assaulted by the Republican front-runner's surrogate. She offered iffy evidence for her allegations. Fields had scrummed Trump. She was too close for comfort to a candidate who is the target of daily death threats. Solemnly, conservatives took to debating the "assault" endured by Fields and the merits of a legal remedy.

The law is an ass. But so are these conservatives. (The Fields matter has since been settled: Megyn Kelly will get Fields a spread in *Vogue*, Kelly's *alma mater*.)

Which brings me to gender: New Conservatives will debate as hotly as any Democrat girl whether something is or isn't "sexist." Feminized discourse, conducted in fretful falsettos by men in trendy eye wear, is now as pervasive on the Right—and certainly as "conservative"—as the cause of women in combat.

Political Correctness: Like liberals, New Conservatives form a party of "isms," not individualism. Diligently do they dissect controversial speech for signs of the dread sexism, racism, ageism. Mainstream conservatives seldom recuse themselves from the act of policing speech or inventing Orwellian linguistic mutations. As an example you have Cornell Williams Brooks (radical leftist, head of National Association for the Advancement of Colored People) and S.E. Cupp (unsharpened pencil, self-styled, "conservative"), both accusing Trump of "otherizing" other people. (Tautology? Circularity? WTF?)

Other defining issues over which New Cons and liberals practically converge:

Multiculturalism is America's strength, but Europe's weakness.

Islam is peaceful, except for a few bad Abduls.

Crime and race. Very important. Old Rightists would have defended Hillary Clinton's 1996 statement about predatory youth. By virtue of having no conscience, no empathy, some kids can be called super predators, she reasoned. "We can talk about why they ended up that way, but first, we have to bring them to heel."

The fact that media still ignore America's perennial race riots and their signature sock-it-to-cracker knockout game; the fact that the press and the pols have rechristened the perps as "teens letting off steam," "juveniles," "unruly youths," "unaccompanied young people"—this does nothing to alter the veracity of the Old Mrs. Clinton's strident, coherent position on violent offenders.

Not unlike Black Lives Matter, conservatives currently admonish the Old Hillary—you guessed—for her racism.

You get the drift. Conservative talk is not all it's cut out to be. When it comes to philosophical convictions (the stuff discussed above), most powerful conservatives more closely resemble their beltway liberal friends than they do Republican Party voters.

From the country's dismal finances and propagandized population, a sizable segment has concluded that conservative power-brokers and liberal power-brokers are indistinguishable.

The problem with Trump is not that he speaks unconservatively, but that he talks incoherently.

"I'm the only one on this stage who's hired people, full stop!'" Trump once thundered. Judging from the repetitive phrases and undeveloped ideas Trump repeats, the singularly gifted people Trump promised to hire have yet to materialize.

Hillary Clinton can talk the hind legs off a donkey. Time to hire talent, Mr. Trump, to help shape a cogent message.

In hiring epistolary and policy talent, Mr. Trump should steer clear of all neoconservatives. In Miami, Mr. Trump rattled off a list of army brass he may hire. He mentioned Colonel Jack H. Jacobs, an honorable man who's not a warmonger (and thus unknown to Fox News viewers).

Luring the only decent Democrat currently in public life to a Trump administration may prove strategic, in scooping up Bernie Sanders' voters. Being a Democrat generally comes with the presumption of asininity, which is why Representative Tulsi Gabbard of Hawaii is unusual. She's an Iraq War veteran, who serves on the Armed Services and Foreign Affairs Committees. She's poised, articulate, beautiful—and she never whinges like Michelle Fields. Gabbard stands firm against gratuitous wars, opposes the deposing of Bashar al-Assad, and despises Debbie Wasserman Schultz, scheming Democratic National Committee Chair and handmaiden to Hillary.

Experienced hand Ed Rollins is a tough conservative strategist. He ought to be tapped by Trump. Another Old-Right conservative is the ever scrappy, always brilliant populist Patrick J. Buchanan, who was Trump before Trump. He'll be indispensable if Trump is to explain to a sissified generation that Trump Nation will not cower before the Alinskyite activists who're trying to silence the hitherto Silent Majority and sunder its right to peaceful assembly.

Self-defense is righteous, not violent. Pacifism is for pinkos.

Ann Coulter's *Adios America*, a book that details how mass immigration is killing America (as Bill O'Reilly would say, or still will), launched the Trump revolution. Ms. Coulter writes pellucid prose. She and Pat should help The Donald craft the rationale for a moratorium on America's legal, million-migrant-a-year, immigration policy. For as I wrote in "The Immigration Scene" (April 28, 2006), "the exclusive emphasis in the immigration debate on border security has helped open-border evangelists immeasurably. Everyone (and his dog) currently concurs that we have no issue with legal immigration, only with the illegal variety. It's now mandatory to pair an objection to the invasion of the American Southwest with an embrace of all forms of legal immigration. The sole emphasis on border security has, in all likelihood, entrenched the *status quo*—Americans will never assert their right to determine the nature of the country they live in and, by extension, the kind of immigrants they welcome. The security risk newcomers pose is the only permissible topic for conversation." Needed is a restoration of pre-1965 thinking to back before Ted Kennedy lied America into multicultural immolation by immigration. Because of Ted, one in five people residing in the U.S. is a foreigner, with next to no English. Because of Ted, Americans are aliens in their own homeland.

(With great power comes great responsibility. Ms. Coulter will have to accept responsibility if a gold-plated wall goes up on the southern border. She'll also have to atone if the borderland along Mexico comes to resemble Liberace's backyard.)

The destruction of this country's social fabric has never bothered liberals. But what of its natural environment? Roy Beck and his NumbersUSA outfit could assist Mr. Trump in making environmentalists aware of the impact of an annual influx of 2-3 million people (counting the illegal intake), on the country's ecosystems, animate and inanimate.

~March 18, 2016

24. WRONG, DONALD TRUMP, ISLAM LOVES US … TO BITS

"I think Islam hates us," said Donald J. Trump days before the last, March 10 debate in Coral Gables, Miami.

To mainstream media, this was a body blow as big as the blasts at the Brussels airport and metro station, on March 22.

The debate moderator gave Trump room to retract. Or, rather, to furnish the religion-of-peace politically correct pieties supplied by John Kasich before Brussels, and Hillary Clinton after the latest murder-by-Muslim of thirty-one European innocents.

The Kasich-Clinton statements are interchangeable:

"Let's be clear: Islam is not our adversary. Muslims are peaceful and tolerant people and have nothing whatsoever to do with terrorism."

Trump plowed on. To the question, "Did you mean all … Muslims?" he replied by insisting that a large number of Islam's 1.6 billion-strong nation—Ummah—are prepared, even poised, to "use very, very harsh means" against Americans, whom, oddly, he, Donald Trump, would dearly like to protect.

"*They're* talking about radical Islamic terrorism or radical Islam," said Trump. "*But* I will tell you this. There's something going on that maybe you don't know about, maybe a lot of other people don't know about."

It's in the "they" and the "but." Trump, whose pronouns are often missing a subject, was likely questioning the competition's habit of pairing "radical" with "Islamic terrorism." For if Islam is radical, as he probably suspects, then the "radical" adjectival is redundant.

People are pacified by such pairings. They persist in using veiled language. We're up against an "ideology," they noodle. We have to fight the ISIS "ideology"—which happens to be the al-Qaida "ideology"; is the "ideology" shared by Boko Haram and the Al-Nusra front; and has been the "ideology" around which Islam has organized since the 7th century, without meaningful religious reformation.

The ISIS "ideology" "represents the natural and inevitable outgrowth of a faith that is given over to hate on a massive scale," writes National Review Online's David French. Surveys conducted across the Muslim world reveal that a majority of Muslims are virulent anti-Semites, those "far removed from the Arab–Israeli conflict" as well.

Well, of course. The vilest vitriol in the Qur'an is reserved for us Jewish "apes."

"Enormous numbers of Muslims are terrorist sympathizers," observes French. "Roughly 50 million" are sympathetic to ISIS. "In Britain, for example, more Muslims join ISIS than join the British army." Overwhelmingly, the Muslims questioned held disgusting views. How can they not? "Polygamy and sexual slavery" (verse 4:3) and the violent subjugation of women (4:34) are commanded in their Holy Book, too.

Brian Kilmeade, a Fox News Channel personality—with all the cerebral deficiencies the affiliation portends—wrote a book, *Thomas Jefferson and the Tripoli Pirates: The Forgotten War That Changed American History*. In it, to judge by a Factor interview he gave, late in 2015, Kilmeade co-opted Jefferson as a neocon, fighting 21st century America's War On Terror.

Kilmeade's silliest pronouncement during that interview was to say that the Muslim Tripoli Pirates had been practicing Islam *in the way it was not meant to be practiced.*

Did the Tripoli Pirates pirate The Authentic Islam, Mr. Kilmeade? If so, when in the course of its bloody history does The Authentic Islam kick-in?

Delve into the Qur'an, the Hadith and the Sira, and it becomes abundantly clear: Islam is radical, has been for some time.

Robert Spencer of Jihad Watch reacted to Trump's truism by excerpting dozens of Qur'anic verses, mandating eternal hatred and contempt for the Infidel. More materially, the faithful are to act on that hatred.

In reading the ghoulish litany, you lose count of the variations on the theme of, "Fight unbelievers until Islam reigns supreme" and make "wide slaughter among them." Spencer then qualifies why Trump is right about the difficulties in separating out radicals from the rest. Muslims have yet to do this themselves. It's their job: "There is no institutional distinction between Muslims who reject jihad terror and those who embrace it."

True to type, the *Christian Science Monitor* has tried to discredit Brigitte Gabriel's estimate of the number of Muslims raring to "cast into the hearts of the unbelievers terror" (3:151). The liberal newspaper ended up bolstering the activist's case. One percent of Europe's Muslim population would likely be willing to turn on Europeans. That's a roiling reservoir of 325,000 Muslims, each capable of "slay[ing] idolaters" (9:5), à la Brussels and Paris (November, 2015).

Idiot alert: A small percentage of a huge number is still a bloody big deal.

So while most Muslims are not terrorists, a hell of a lot of them are ready, willing and able to dabble in the life-style.

You say, "There are some rough passages in the Hebrew Testament, too."

Indeed. But they do not apply to anyone any longer— unless, in the words of Mr. Spencer, "you happen to be a Hittite, Girgashite, Amorite, Canaanite Perizzite, Hivite, or Jebusite." Unsuited to obedience, we Jews have always argued over, interpreted and reinterpreted our holy texts.

A principled non-interventionist must be first to concede that America's adventurous foreign policy is *a necessary* condition for Muslim aggression; it is, however, far from *a sufficient* one. (Irrespectively, Americans don't deserve to die stateside because of their government's actions abroad.)

"Islam's borders are bloody and so are its innards," stated one of America's most brilliant writers, Samuel P.

Huntington, author of *The Clash of Civilizations and the Remaking of World Order.* "The fundamental problem is not Islamic fundamentalism. It is Islam," he argued, in 1998. Islam is "a different civilization whose people are convinced of the superiority of their culture and are obsessed with the inferiority of their power."

And Islam counsels *conquest*, not *coexistence*. Islamic terrorism is thus the handiwork of people who've *heeded*, not *hijacked*, the unreformed Islam.

A President Trump ought to be able to keep his promise and stem the annual influx of 100,000 Muslims (multiplied many times due to family unification and chain migration policies, which allow one qualified sponsor to bring in a tribe).

Legal scholars of the caliber of Eugene Volokh and Eric Posner have reluctantly admitted that a moratorium on, or cessation of, Muslim immigration is not necessarily unconstitutional, under the "plenary power doctrine."

States the federal law:

> Whenever the president finds that the entry of any aliens or of any class of aliens into the United States would be detrimental to the interests of the United States, he may by proclamation, and for such period as he shall deem necessary, suspend the entry of all aliens or any class of aliens as immigrants or nonimmigrants, or impose on the entry of aliens any restrictions he may deem to be appropriate.

Wrong, Donald Trump, Islam Loves Us... To Bits

All Muslims can thrive in America. Not all Americans will thrive in the presence of Muslims. This is because the faith of Muslims is Islam. And Islam predisposes to violence.

A preponderance of Muslims will remain dormant. But they could be "triggered" at any time, as was the case with Khalid and Brahim El Bakraoui. It only took this duo and a culprit or two to extinguish thirty lives and maim and mutilate hundreds more.

Brussels' brothers El Bakraoui have "contributed" as much to their adopted country, Belgium, as Boston's Tsarnaev brothers have to America.

American public policy is not a program to benefit the world; nor is it a means to a diplomatic end—namely appeasing the Muslim partners of Kasich and Rubio. Law must minimize aggregate harm. Sensible, reality bound libertarians will embrace Popperian minimal harm, rather than Benthamite maximum happiness. U.S. public policy must, very plainly, keep Americans safe without aggressing against others.

Since humanity does not have an inherent, natural right to venture wherever, whenever—stopping Muslim mass migration into the U.S. is not in violate of humanity's natural rights.

~March 25, 2016

25. APRIL FIELDS' DAY: MICHELLE FOOL & JOURNALISM'S FEMINIZATION

In the 1990s, broadcaster Charles Sykes wrote an important book called *A Nation Of Victims: The Decay of the American Character*.

Fast forward to 2016, and Mr. Sykes is defending a character on grounds he once rejected in his trailblazing book.

When Mr. Sykes lamented the "The Decay of the American Character," no reader was under the impression it was the mettle of reporter Michelle Fields he was hankering for and hoping to see restored.

I've watched the grainy footage that has fueled the hysterics of Ms. Fields and her shameful sisterhood, domesticated males included. The whole world has watched. In it, Donald Trump can be clearly observed recoiling defensively, as Ms. Fields presses up against him. Invisible to the naked eye was the assault Fields alleges.

Still, if Hillary Clinton's flesh were being pressed by a reporter like Fields, and sidekick Huma Abedin forcefully flicked the reporter aside, I'd say the same. No assault occurred. No litigation should follow. Leave Huma the heck alone.

In other words, a reasonable individual can easily accept—even in the absence of visual evidence—that a protective campaign manager, former cop Corey Lewandowski, might have instinctively shoved the pushy reporter away from Mr. Trump.

To frame this melee as an assault and manufacture a national incident is beneath contempt; is disgraceful. Unacceptable is that the law rushed to validate Fields' hurt feelings by charging Lewandowski with a misdemeanor battery.

As unacceptable was the reaction of Ms. Fields and her solipsistic sisters—those with the Y chromosome included. Ms. Fields is not a victim and her conduct demonstrates decay of character.

Were she a reasonable professional, Ms. Fields would've grasped that there was no intention to harm her; only to protect a man who is in constant, real danger. (A bruised massive ego aside, Fields was unharmed.)

Mr. Trump is the object of unparalleled death threats and hatred. If someone moves you aside in a journalistic scrum; it's because they perceive you to be a threat to such a man.

What would a pro have done? Step back. Take five. Shrug it off. Or give the grabber a piece of her mind.

Better still, Ms. Fields, call CNN's heroic war correspondent Arwa Damon for perspective. If this recipient of the Courage in Journalism Award doesn't reply because under fire, give Clarissa Ward a tinkle in Syria. Raise your staccato tart-like voice. Those bombs are loud.

Look: Michelle Fields and her enablers are no conservatives. These women and their male helpers inhabit a solipsistic, narcissistic, decidedly progressive universe. In *A Nation Of Victims*, Mr. Sykes had described a lamentable process whereby America's formative institutions had morphed from transmitting timeless values, to being propelled by a therapeutic ethos, a "social contract with The Self."

A contract with The Self—or the selfie—better describes the new breed of badly bred, unprofessional, Michelle Fields millenials.

The woman's claims-making is that of someone who sees herself as the center of a small universe, pussy-whipped, feminized and sissified by her ilk.

The same goes for the empaneled female screeches who've come to her rescue, and are seen on anti-Trump TV, baying in unison for the blood of Messrs. Trump and Lewandowski. (At least two of the phony conservative females who've detected a crime against Fields—S. E. Cupp and Meghan McCain—are borderline retarded.)

The Sykes book I devoured in the 1990s would never have countenanced such unbecoming conduct; would never have demanded that a man be brought to heel for defending an imperiled presidential candidate. Now, the New Mr. Sykes was asserting that a real man would apologize to a woman.

Did Sykes mean to say a real man would cop to a physical assault he did not commit, based on a woman's say-so?

April Field's Day: Michelle Fool & Journalism's Feminization

No! Real men affirm reality. The immutable reality is that no assault occurred. Therefore, no litigation should follow.

I don't know how the law got to a place where it considers it a crime to shove an individual aside so as to maintain a perimeter around a man, Mr. Trump, who is the object of death threats.

I do know that law is force. Whenever a lawmaker legislates, he creates more potential criminals out of individuals whose actions were once—still are—naturally licit.

Our venerated legal system locks up more people per 100,000 individuals than do China and Russia, respectively. Yet look at the U.S. Constitution. The Constitution is remarkable in its brevity. The laws under which free men were meant to live and thrive are few and fundamental.

That Mr. Lewandowski is being criminalized and his employer maligned for an infraction invisible to the naked eye tells me something is very wrong with the law. The same can be said for the culture. The contagion whipped-up by Ms. Fields and her coven of pseudo-conservatives should repulse any conservative-minded man or woman, irrespective of his or her feelings about Mr. Trump.

The assault on Ms. Fields was as real as the ectoplasm said to spill from a medium's mouth during séance (which is to say, as truthful as what comes out of Megyn Kelly's mouth).

~April 1, 2016

26. TRUMP VS. THE BANANA REPUBLICANS

There's a difference between (small r) republican principles and the Republican Party's rules of procedure. But *National Review* neoconservative Jonah Goldberg doesn't see it.

Or, maybe Goldberg is using America's founding, governing principles to piggyback the Republican Party's oft revised and rigged rules to respectability.

Conservatives who harbor the quaint expectation that voters, not party operatives, would choose the nominee stand accused by Goldberg of fetishizing unfiltered democracy.

"America is a republic not a simple democracy," says Goldberg, in motivating for Grand Old Party chicanery.

Goldberg's argument is a cunning but poor one. It confuses bureaucratic rules with higher principles: the republicanism of America's Constitution makers.

Through a Bill of Rights and a scheme that divides authority between autonomous states and a national government, American federalism aimed to secure the rights of the individual by imposing strict limits on the power of thumping majorities and a central government.

The Goldberg variations on republicanism won't wash (with apologies to the sublime J.S. Bach, who is rolling in his grave). The Republican Party's arbitrary rules relate to the Founding Founders' republicanism as the Romney Rule relates to veracity.

The Romney initiated Rule 40(b) is a recent addition to the Republican Party rule book. It stipulates that in order to win the nomination, a candidate must demonstrate he has earned a majority of delegates from at least eight different states. Rule 40 (b) was passed *post-haste* to thwart libertarian candidate Ron Paul.

Party crooks and their lawyers now find themselves in a pickle, because Governor John Kasich, candidate for the establishment (including the *New York Times* and the Huffington Post), has yet to meet the Republican rule *du jour*.

So, what do The Rulers do? They plan to change the rules. Again.

Pledged delegates are not supposed to act as autonomous agents. Their voting has to be tethered to the candidate whom voters have overwhelmingly chosen. But not when The Party parts company with The Voters. Then, delegates might find themselves unmoored from representing the voters.

Republican National Committee Chairman Reince Priebus has hinted at allowing pledged delegates the freedom to betray their pledge.

No doubt, the villainous Ben Ginsberg, the Romney campaign's chief counsel, will be called on to facilitate the Faustian bargain. Ginsberg lewdly revealed to a repulsed crew at MSNBC how he could make mischief with Trump's delegates, during the "pre-convention" wheeling-and-dealing stage, much as he did with Ron Paul's delegates. Host Rachel Maddow—she's vehemently opposed—appeared both fascinated and appalled, as were her co-hosts.

Republican Party apparatchiks have always put The Party over The People and The People are on to them. Still, most media—with the laudable exceptions of the aforementioned MSNBC election-coverage team and Sean Hannity—have united to portray the Republican Party apparatus as an honest broker on behalf of the Republican voter. (Indeed, the "dreaded" Donald has forced some unlikely partners to slip between the sheets together.)

In truth, the GOP is a tool of scheming operatives, intent on running a candidate of their own choosing.

The sheer force of Trump, however, is deforming this political organ out of shape. The Trump Force is exposing for all to see the ugly underbelly of the GOP and its delegate system. As party rules go, an American may cast his vote for a candidate, only to have a clever party functionary finagle the voter out of his vote.

Too chicken to admit this to Mr. Hannity's face, Reince Priebus has said as much to friendlies like Wisconsin radio host Charlie Sykes (who's having a moment).

Priebus has finally seconded what his lieutenants have been telling media all along: "This is a nomination for the Republican Party. If you don't like the party," then tough luck. "The party is choosing a nominee."

Before Priebus came out as a crook, there was popular Nebraska Republican Senator Ben Sasse. As a "real" conservative, Sasse would like nothing more than to dissolve the Republican voter base and elect another, more compliant segment of supporters, to better reflect his ideas (a sentiment floated, in 1953, by Stalinist playwright Bertolt Brecht, when East Berliners revolted against their Communist Party bosses).

Sasse phrased his goals more diplomatically:

"The American people deserve better than two fundamentally dishonest New York liberals" (Mr. Trump and Hillary Clinton).

It fell, again, to MSNBC's Chuck Todd to put Sasse on the spot:

> Let me ask you this. If you have—what is a political party? And I ask it this way. Is it a, is it a party who [sic] gets its principles and its ideals from its leaders, or is it ground up? What if this is the people speaking and the people are basically handing the nomination to Trump? You may not like it, but is it then fundamentally that the Republican party is changing because the people that are members of it have changed?

Sasse, who speaks the deceptive language of fork-tongued conservatives so much better than Trump, conceded that "a political party is a tool, not a religion," but went on, nevertheless, to dictate his terms to the base:

"Find the right guy." Trump's not it.

Exposed by the force of the Trump uprising, this is the ugly, Republican, elections-deciding system. The

Constitution has nothing to do with it. Decency and fairness are missing from it. And crooks abound in it.

Prattle about who is and who's not an authentic conservative is redundant if you're a crook fixing to steal the nomination.

Prattle about "we are just following The Rules, The Rules are the rule" is plain eerie. When in history did we hear a riff on that theme before? Not to invoke the invalid *Argumentum ad Hitlerum*, which would be terribly wrong—even in the context of the GOP—but when Republicans refer to the Rules of The Republican Party as their source of moral authority; it doesn't sound good and it isn't good.

Contra Goldberg, this enervating Party Machine—operating on state, national and conventional levels—relates to small 'r' republicanism as the Republican Party rulebook relates to the U.S. Constitution: not at all.

Party Rules have no constitutional imprimatur.

In a banana republic, despots deploy crude tactics to retain power. Banana Republicans are similar, except they hide behind a complex electoral process, maneuvered by high-IQ crooks.

~April 8, 2016

27. TRUMP'S AMERICA FIRST POLICY: REMARKABLY SOPHISTICATED

"Unsophisticated rambling," "simplistic," "reckless."

The verdict about Donald J. Trump's foreign policy, unveiled after his five-for-five victory in Pennsylvania, Maryland, Delaware, Rhode Island and Connecticut, was handed down by vested interests: members of the military-media-think tank complex. People like Former Secretary of State Madeleine Albright. People Dwight Eisenhower counseled against, in his farewell address to the nation:

In the councils of government, we must guard against the acquisition of unwarranted influence, whether sought or unsought, by the military-industrial complex.

Naturally, Albright wants U.S. foreign policy to remain complex, convoluted; based not on bedrock American principles, but on bureaucratically friendly talking points, imbibed in the "best" schools of government, put to practice by the likes of the Council on Foreign Relations.

Like so many D.C. insiders who move seamlessly between government and the flush-with-funds think-tank industry, Albright has worked for CFR. (Yearly revenue: $61 million. Mission: Not America First.)

Neo-Wilsonian foreign policy is big business.

Wait for the Brookings Institution, RAND Corporation and the Center for American Progress to pile on Trump's "unsophisticated," America-centric foreign policy—especially now that the Republican Party's presumptive nominee has signaled his intention to get the U.S. "out of the nation-building business."

Like an invasive Kudzu, these anti-American forces are everywhere. What Trump's advocating translates into a reduced profile for them: less demand for their neo-Wilsonian schemes, promulgated in focused blindness by think tank types and by most tele-tarts.

Reduced demand for American agitation abroad will mean fewer "media references per year," less "monthly traffic" to monetize on websites, less influence in the halls of power and, ultimately, reduced revenues.

We might even see fewer color-coded revolutions around the world.

Trump's promised change to American foreign policy can't sit well with the International Republican Institute (IRI), the National Democratic Institute (NDI) and Freedom House. These have been described by the press as "Washington-based group[s] that promote democracy and open elections."

More like Alinskyite agitators.

The IRI and the NDI are excrescences of the Republican and Democratic Parties, respectively. As Trump supporters know, on the foreign-policy front, not much distinguishes America's duopoly. Republicans and Democrats work in tandem, Saul-Alinsky style, to bring about volcanic transformation in societies that desperately need stability. Or, as Trump put it, "We tore up what institutions they had and then were surprised at what we unleashed."

CNN is right to fret that the Trump foreign policy address delivers "little in the way of a recognizable foreign strategy."

Fear not, CNN. Trump's promise to pursue "peace and prosperity, not war"—the candidate's commitment that, "unlike other candidates, war and aggression will not be [his] first instinct"—is recognizable to those whose loved ones have returned in body bags, from the blighted and benighted territories into which Trump adversaries want to keep tunneling.

Evidently, victims of liberal interventionism and neoconservative global democratic crusades think putting Americans first is a wildly sophisticated idea.

Ordinary, patriotic Americans have been hoodwinked by these sophisticates into sacrificing their children to Madeleine Albright's Moloch.

It would appear these Trump supporters and America's soldiers no longer wish to throw beautiful young lives to the think-tank industry's God of War.

"Trump's foreign policy platform would dismantle the post-World War II architecture so lovingly built up by the War Party and its congressional Myrmidons," posits Justin Raimondo, editor at Antiwar.com. "This is why he's made all the right enemies ... Trump's triumph would mark the end of the neocons as a viable political force on the Right."

Amen Selah.

It's by no means axiomatic, moreover, that "defense treaties and overseas bases that emerged after World War II still serve U.S. interests," confessed policy analyst Rosa Brooks.

As with any bureaucracy, NATO, the North Atlantic Treaty Organization, is good for those it employs; bad for The People who must pay for it and tolerate its self-perpetuating policies and sinecured politicians forever after.

NATO, conceded the *Washington Post*, was "formed to fight the Soviet Union. ... The USSR evaporated a quarter-century ago." Like a zombie, this segment of the international superstate "has lurched along, taking on new roles."

The establishment, Left and Right, equates *what governments do* with what *the people need*.

Take CNN's Christiane Amanpour. In ways intellectual, the anchor is impoverished. She is, however, never poor. Amanpour's net worth is $12.5 Million. She has lived, loved and worked among the upper echelons her entire life, including in her birth place of Iran. Terribly privileged, Amanpour is more authentically *Shahs of Sunset* than an ordinary American.

The CNN personality has ridiculed Trump's "poor me America" routine. She disputes his tack about a weakened America whose exploiters should "pony up." Simply put, said Trump, "Our allies are not paying their fair share." "We have spent trillions over time ... provid[ing] a strong defense for Europe and Asia":

> The countries we are defending must pay for the
> cost of this defense, and, if not, the U.S. must be
> prepared to let these countries defend
> themselves. We have no choice.

When Trump challenged America's continued
membership in NATO, shysters like Amanpour, Ted Cruz
too, cupped hands to claim the charity of the gullible
American people. They "argued" that we need to continue
to give over two percent of GDP to keep this welfare-
warfare elephantiasis going.

Their error—Amanpour's error—is to collapse the
distinction between America (overall, relatively wealthy)
and *individual Americans*, legions of whom are dirt poor and
desperate.

But businessman Trump makes no such mistake. He
can't help but put Americans first.

The Donald's foreign policy *coup de grâce*: "Under a
Trump Administration, no American citizen will ever again
feel that their needs come second to the citizens of foreign
countries."

"Our foreign policy goals must be based on America's
core national security interests," he asserted, as he "pledged
to ... focus on stability in the [Middle East and the region],
not on nation-building." Recognizing the differences
America has with China and Russia, he also vowed to 'seek
common ground based on shared interests.'"

"My goal is to establish a foreign policy that will endure for several generations centered on prioritizing America first."

Remarkably, our foreign-policy, maze-bright rats see this Trump stance as unsophisticated.

To the contrary: Trump's foreign policy evinces a sophisticated understanding of the role of government in the lives of a free people.

The duty of the "night-watchman state of classical-liberal theory" is primarily to its own. The classical liberal government's duty is to its own citizens, first.

As Americans, we have a solemn, negative, leave-them-alone duty not to violate the rights of foreigners everywhere to life, liberty and property.

We have no duty to uphold their rights. Why so? Because (ostensibly) upholding the negative rights of the world's citizens involves compromising the negative liberties of Americans—inalienable American lives, liberties and livelihoods.

By promising to "never send our finest into battle, unless necessary," Trump demonstrates a visceral, critical understanding that an American president is obligated to defend—he dare not squander!—the lives of Americans. He thus comes closest to fulfilling the executive duties of an American leader.

~ April 29, 2016

28. SOMEONE SHOULD TELL BILL KRISTOL DWARF TOSSING IS CRUEL

Prominent neoconservative Bill Kristol shared his election-year hallucinations with the nation. From the ashes of the Republican primaries would rise a man to stand for president against victor Donald J. Trump, a Sisyphean task that has been attempted and failed by seventeen other worthies.

This individual is David French, an attorney, a decorated Iraq War veteran, and writer for the decidedly "Against Trump" *National Review*. Curiously, Kristol's independent candidate is a "devout social conservative," an evangelical who questions the merits of "de-stigmatizing" homosexuality, rejects the progressive premise upon which the transgender, potty wars are being waged, and would keep women out of combat.

Why, then, would a "relatively secular faction within the Republican Party," the neoconservatives, make common cause with the Party's fundamentalist wing? Jeet Heer, senior editor at *New Republic*, asks this question—a riddle familiar to students and scholars of American conservatism.

The alliance or, rather, the master-servant relationship between neoconservatives and the Religious Right is an old one. Political evangelists have long since been brought to heel by the Washington-based neoconservatives. "Most on the Religious Right have hardly resisted such cooptation, having perhaps nowhere to go financially, politically or professionally," wrote Dr. Paul Gottfried in *The Conservative Movement*, his prophetic, 1993 forensic examination of the roots of the conservative crack-up.

French is vested in an aggressive, expansionist foreign policy. His impressive military credentials, in his role as a tool of democratic internationalism, are meant to provide a stark contrast to Trump's nativism. At least as Kristol sees it.

French is not an American Firster in the way Donald Trump is. For a man can don the uniform and fight Caesar's wars, but that doesn't necessarily make him someone who puts his country first—unless one conflates the interests and well-being of ordinary Americans with wars of choice plotted by the New York-Washington axis of power. This error is not one Mr. Trump commits. While the presumptive Republican Party's nominee clearly has great affection for America's veterans, he doesn't love all the wars they've been ordered to fight.

Leave it to Hillary Clinton and Mr. Kristol to collapse the distinction between spreading democratic values around the world (their way) and acting in the national interest (Trumps' way).

As much as he abhors Trump's America First chauvinism, Kristol ought to have realized by now that Trump won his primary fight by standing for Middle-American populism and American interests, as against the establishment Right's internationalism. How many more "professional Republicans" will the political elites toss at Trump?

This political blood sport is becoming as degrading to all parties as dwarf tossing.

Concessions to the Religious Right notwithstanding, Heer maintains that the Libertarian Party's "Gary Johnson-Bill Weld ticket looks like a much more credible anti-Trump force on the right" for Kristol to consider.

From the perspective of this writer, a long-time libertarian, however, the mindset of the two goofballs aforementioned by Heer is more statist and deferential to state structures than Trump's.

In an interview with CNN's Victor Blackwell, Weld, in particular, voiced objections thoroughly statist to the various policies Trump was proposing.

> Weld: Some of the stuff that he's running on I think is absolutely chaotic. I'm going to do this to Mexico. OK, that's a violation of the North American Free Trade agreement, which is the supreme law of the land. It is a treaty. We signed it. I'll do this to China. No questions asked. OK, that's a violation of the World Trade Organization rules exposing us, the United States, to sanctions. And we would be the rogue nation. I don't think we want to be the rogue nation. You know? Let's let North Korea be the rogue nation, not us.

By Weld's telling, Trump must refrain from doing what he has proposed to do lest he violate this or the other agreement between the U.S. government and various supranational systems, which Weld treats as holy writ.

Granted, radical libertarians will contend that the Constitution itself is the thin edge of the wedge that has allowed successive U.S. governments to cede the rights of Americans to these suprastate systems. Specifically, the "Supremacy Clause" in Article VI states that all treaties made by the national government shall be "the supreme Law of the Land," and shall usurp the laws of the states.

Either way, all libertarian-minded conservatives who yearn to breathe free should want the chains with which others have bound Americans dissolved. Johnson and Weld object to Trump renegotiating agreements or optimizing them for Americans, on the statist grounds that to so do would violate agreements that by their nature sideline the American people. Smashing or refashioning these agreements and reclaiming national, state and individual sovereignty, as Trump proposes, is certainly more libertarian than the Johnson-Weld worldview allows.

On this front, the dissident Right—Trump's right-wing populists and right-thinking libertarians—ought to agree.

Someone should tell Bill Kristol and his neoconservatives it's time to quit tossing dwarfs at Donald Trump. Dwarf tossing is cruel.

~ June 3, 2016

29. TESTOSTERONE, GOING, GOING, ALMOST GONE ...

There are only two men in the 2016 presidential race: Hillary Clinton and Donald Trump.

Like or dislike her, there's no questioning Hillary's manly *bona fides*. Mrs. Clinton is as tough as she's philosophically misguided.

At the first Democratic debate, on October 14, 2015, Bernie Sanders, Martin O'Malley and Lincoln Chafee shuffled meekly to their respective podiums.

Only Jim Webb and Mrs. Clinton strode onto the stage like soldiers.

(Media reached for the smelling salts when Webb, who's hardly gung-ho for war, professed to have killed a man or two in battle. They prefer a technocrat like Hillary, who specializes in sending men to war, to a warrior like Webb who understands why wars must be avoided.)

Unless her handlers coach her on acting femininely, you'll never catch Hillary blubbering about Bill and Chelsey coming first in her life.

She doesn't!

They don't (come first)!

No, siree. For Hillary, it's ambition before family.

It's true that in her door-stopper of a book, *Hard Choices*, Hillary shared her womanly desire to be a steward of the world, revealing that the birth of granddaughter Charlotte awakened in Grandma Clinton a yen to weave a protective, world-wide web for baby Charlotte and her generation. But that was just Hillary using Charlotte to disguise her own hegemonic aspirations.

Mighty Mouse

When Hillary expects it to pay political dividends, she fights like a girl, claws drawn.

Her April 19 victory in the New York primary could hardly be bettered. But it's unlikely to soften Mrs. Clinton's sharpshooting. She and rival Bernie Sanders have been locked in a cycle of sorts, where Sanders will try mightily to stand up to Hillary, and she'll swat him down like a fly.

During his March 2011 appearance on the defunct Dylan Ratigan Show, the senator from Vermont had fighting words about the misadventure in Libya: "We have lost thousands of lives in Afghanistan and Iraq and trillions of dollars … I am not enthusiastic about the U.S. getting into yet another conflict given the other two wars and $14 trillion in national debt."

Five years on, and Sanders is too petrified to lay the ruination of Libya at Hillary's sturdy feet. Hillary and her She Warlords cracked the whip at Foggy Bottom. From the invasion to the fiasco of Benghazi; Clinton, Samantha Power and Susan Rice guided that intervention. But Sanders has only to recount the ambient horrors of Hillary's foreign policy—the vote for "the disastrous war in Iraq," for one—

and Mrs. Clinton's Amazon Warriors at CNN and elsewhere crow, "Is Bernie Sanders taking the low road?"

It's a little late in the game, but April saw Bernie try his utmost to expose Mrs. Clinton's record for all to see. His thundering, "Hillary Clinton isn't qualified to be president," however, soon gave way to a whimper, a squeak, a "she started it"; "I would have preferred an issue-oriented campaign." Mumble-mumble. "Where's my mommy?"

Sanders finally settled on, "I question her judgment, not experience." The senator was soon bowing-and-scraping again because a surrogate attached the words "corporate Democratic whores" to Hillary's incremental approach to socializing the medical means of production. (Yes, Sanders' Fabian fondness for the state, economic planning and centralization exceeds Hillary's.)

Sanders' resistance in the face of ruthless machine politics mounted on behalf of Clinton by Democratic National Committee Chair Debbie Wasserman Schultz has been flaccid. At the same time, the senator has been fierce in his defense of Hillary's email security breaches as secretary of state. He famously fought off Hillary's critics, neutering himself with this zinger:

"The American people are sick and tired [of] hearing about your damn emails."

Compared to battle-axe Clinton, Sanders is a mouse, not a man.

Early in March, The Mouse scolded The Man for interrupting him. Said the timid Sanders, "Excuse me, I'm talking." Right away, the gynocentric national media erupted in a "debate" that revolved around a preposterous proposition:

Was poor Bernie sexist?

Of course, Methuselah jumps to attention whenever Hillary reprimands him for his failure to stand by President Barack Obama on gun control.

And who can forget when, in August of 2015, socialist-in-Seattle Sanders skedaddled as a couple of girl protesters got in his face and grabbed his microphone?

Don't let Hillary's "wife, mom, grandma" routine fool you. That's her Twitter handle; that's not her.

You sense that if she had her way, Hillary would ditch the familial shtick. But Hill's a smart cookie; she goes through the "wife, mom, grandma" motions because she must.

Unlike the mucho Hillary, some other "men" racing for the White House have successfully "transitioned," as Caitlyn Jenner would say.

Don't Do The Thymus Thump

Guess who caught hell for sending out a girly, sanctimonious, pity-me fundraising email about the personal sacrifices made by a presidential candidate? Hillary? Donald? Not on your life. Both thrive on the grueling schedule.

The "man" griping about a lack of work-life balance was Ted Cruz.

There's a lot that's phony about Cruz, but it's not his Twitter handle. It identifies him correctly, first, as the "father of two" and "Heidi's husband."

Likewise, on Twitter, the real John Kasich is "husband and dad" before he's "governor of Ohio." Kasich regularly offers group hugs, calls for unity, feigns compassion and begins speeches with gooey references to his daughters.

When Marco Rubio forgot his rehearsed lines, he'd resort to rote references to "my mother, my kids, our kids deserve better."

Obama's one of the girls, too. First up on the president's Twitter handle are the words "dad and husband." The most powerful man in the world, the POTUS, dutifully defers to FLOTUS and family first.

Manifestly ambitious men in their element never used to pretend their ambition didn't inform who they were and what they did. Those are the ways of men molded in the image of woman.

Certainly Donald Trump has never described himself as "husband to Melania, father to Ivanka, grandad to ..."

"President of the greatest country on earth. Bite me," is how a Trump in the White House would likely announce himself on social media.

Other than Governor Chris Christie, who's been eliminated from the running, Mr. Trump is the only Alpha Male among his Republican rivals.

Who endorses Trump? Mucho men do: The Border Patrol Union, Sherriff Joe Arpaio, the race-car drivers' association (NASCAR), the New York Veteran Police

Association, actors Jon Voight and Scott Baio, boxer Mike Tyson, rockers Kid Rock and Ted Nugent, kickass Kirstie Alley.

Anger-Shaming

"I don't like that word," quivered Kasich, when his Super PAC called Mr. Cruz a liar. "It might damage his brand," fretted his groupies in mainstream media. "For the sake of the kids," the governor once pleaded, "please watch the tone; stop the shouting."

Like the women folk who give them their marching orders, Kasich-country hates honest language.

Another trend in America's hopelessly feminized discourse is anger-shaming. This particular female ploy is used (against manly minds) to negate righteous indignation.

After all, forceful speech could very well signal a resolve to pursue unwavering positions. We can't have that! To the women folk—and their obedient males—strong language indicates it's time to restore calm and equilibrium. Anger is bad, they'll intone, while insisting unambiguous words be replaced with words signifying sameness and stasis—tolerance, consensus, unity, openness, inclusiveness.

Tellingly, only Trump has owned his anger. Only Trump has refused to be henpecked.

"I am very angry because our country is being run horribly and I gladly accept the mantle of anger," he roared, as the anger-shaming reached a crescendo.

"He's playing the politics of anger to get a rise out of a crowd" was the consensus on Anderson Cooper 360°, the eponymous show of CNN's Alpha female.

"Donald Trump has brought the party down to a new low. He's feeding off of people's anger about this country on both parties," wailed bloodless Republican Erick Erickson, of Red State fame.

Moaned a Politico writer to MSNB's Kate Snow: "His brand is macho. He bullies. He wields power. He plays to win."

OMG! And what next?!

As to, "Act like a grownup", "Be the adult in the room": Who other than a mother reprimanding a child or henpecking a husband (or Republican strategist Ana Navarro) would use such anemic, prissy clichés?

Hillary would— but *only* to control the men.

One thing seems certain: If nature is allowed to take its course; the showdown on the first Tuesday after the first Monday in November 2016 will be between the two men in the race:

The Hildebeest and The Donald.

The Inevitability Of Eternal Verities, Even Biology

Programed in feminist myth-making, journalists, young and old, have asked incredulously, "Why would western girls travel to join Islamic State fighters?" "ISIS men don't believe in equality between the sexes."

At heart, neither do women. Not when hormones rage.

Brainwashed to think biology is incidental, and that men and women are essentially interchangeable; younger readers will find it harder to grasp something as primordial as the male-female biological category.

One reason girls put on black nose bags and flock to become ISIS brides is that ISIS projects strength. Strength is sexy. Women are biologically programmed to be attracted to powerful men.

Speaking in a deep, sonorous voice; in what sounds like classical Arabic, an imam can be observed on YouTube delivering a sermon from East Jerusalem's Al-Aqsa Mosque. The object of Sheikh Muhammad Ayed's coruscating derision is the emasculated West. It is primed for a muscular, Muslim takeover, he argues.

Said Ayed (as translated by The Middle East Media Research Institute):

> But they have lost their fertility, so they look for fertility in their midst. We will give them fertility! We will breed children with them, because we shall conquer their countries— whether you like it or not, oh Germans, oh Americans, oh French, oh Italians, and all those like you. Take the refugees! We shall soon collect them in the name of the coming Caliphate. We will say to you: These are our

sons. Send them, or we will send our armies to you.

On its side, Islam has ascetic evangelists such as Ayed, who bow to no one and use all the bad words that make Governor Kasich quiver and quake.

On our side we have Father Michael Pfleger! He's the too-hideous-to-behold, standard issue preacher-cum-Obama idolater.

Tell me this: Who looks and sounds more impressive to the young and the impressionable? The impassioned, manly, Muslim imam, in his flowing, Lawrence-of-Arabia robes, who speaks the words of his Prophet? Or, Father Pfleger, the soft face of the West's ultra-liberal faith; a tool of liberal public administration; a man more eager to prostrate himself to Caesar than to serve a higher authority?

Pfleger's ilk are in the four corners of the earth preaching hate for their own kind. Thus, in a week in which fifteen blacks wielding Kalashnikovs killed two white farmers in KwaZulu-Natal; another excuse-for-a-man—man-of-the-cloth Michael Vorster—was at the pulpit puling about the controlling ways of "whiteness."

When a vulnerable Anglo-American boy hears preachers, parents, pedagogues and politicians pound on about our country's Founding Fathers as the archetypical pale, patriarchal oppressors—he quickly learns to reject his country's heritage and look elsewhere for masculine inspiration, maybe even at Muhammad.

Boys, especially, need strong men in their lives—men who affirm their masculinity. American boys, however, are mired in an estrogen-infused, cloistered world, where strong men in authority are an endangered minority.

Religious or irreligious, the generic western guy oozes psychological correctness but not much manliness. He never takes charge; he consults and cooperates. He's not necessarily effeminate, but he's safely androgynous—and most certainly not guy-like in the Trumpian sense. As personalities go, this Generic Guy and his wife (or "life partner") are indistinguishable.

The feminization and regulation of society over decades has meant that life-saving manliness is increasingly confined to corners upon which women are less likely to encroach: the cockpit or combat.

Perhaps this blurring of biological boundaries accounts for why, in Europe, there are no men left to defend the women folk. From Cologne to Hamburg to Stuttgart, the mass molestation of German women by Muslim refugees (hashtag "rapefugees") elicited very little outrage from their natural protectors: the remaining fifty percent of the population.

Why, a decadent dilatant named Ralf Jaeger (interior minister for North Rhine-Westphalia) even ventured that "right-wing poisoning of the climate of our society" is "at least as awful as the acts of those assaulting the women." Father Pfleger and the head of the Roman Catholic Church, Pope Francis, would concur. The last scurried to wash the feet of his Christ-like victims: the refugees, not the raped.

Outside the pigeonhole of politics, the New Breed of Man can be observed in his natural habitat, the supermarket, scrutinizing products for trans fats. Strapped to his sunken chest is a papoose infant carrier. He has a few cranky kids in tow whose outing to the store he'll be laboring to make a "learning experience"; a nightmare for every other patron.

"Old Timers" like Trump, on the other hand, would not be caught dead in such compromising positions. Trumpian fathers lead by example. "Watch me, son. Do as I do." Men in the old mold take their boys to a construction site, not a supermarket. They generally sport deeper voices, a slight swagger that no amount of politically correct bullying can tame, and they do their jobs to the best of their abilities— and in the face of persistent prattle over racism, sexism equal pay for unequal effort, etc.

Socio-Chemical Castration

I've often wondered whether decades of emasculation— legal and cultural—have bred the West's pushover "girly boys."

Data released in 2006 by one Dr. Thomas Travison and colleagues, at the New England Research Institutes in Watertown, Massachusetts, suggested that levels of the male hormone have been dropping precipitously in American men. Testosterone levels have been declining at a rate of one percent a year. American men are indeed losing the stuff that makes them mucho.

Could the feminization of society over the past decades be changing males, body and mind? Could the subliminal stress involved in sublimating one's essential biological nature be producing effeminate, less manly men?

Because they're favored politically, it's fair to say that Muslim-Americans, African-Americans and their interfacing statistical subsets are harassed far less about their manly biological nature. This cohort is also a manifestly manly cohort. I wonder if Muslim-Americans and African-Americans have been similarly affected by declines in testosterone levels. To follow my hypothesis, these sets of politically privileged men should suffer less of a hormonal deficit.

Adjust for differences in aggregate baseline levels of testosterone, then do this politically incorrect scientific study. It might save our boys from the socio-chemical castration they're undergoing.

The hypothalamic-pituitary-adrenal axis is a delicate homeostatic feedback loop, intricately involved in regulating hormones and stress. Has it become the axis of evil in the war on men? Behind the cultural transformation of men by American feminists could lie a hormonal horror story.

Dissolving 'The Constitution Of Man' In The Service Of Sameness

There's more to blunting male-female differences.

Testosterone, Going, Going, Almost Gone ...

The brave new world we inhabit puts a premium on sameness and uniformity of thought. The prototype "individual" in this monochromatic universe is led by the nose. He shares his left-liberal faith with ninety-nine percent of humanity. But because he pierces that easily led proboscis and, say, worships Satan, he stands a good chance of being inducted into the Lisa Ling Hall of Individualism. (Ling is a CNN documentarian who sells her intellectually incurious audiences on the notion that freaky life styles and habits make for a kaleidoscope of individualism, so long as the freaks are liberal.)

Praised by Hillary Clinton as "strong, brave young women," who "refuse to let their voices be silenced," the Russian punk band Pussy Riot is comprised of the detritus of humanity. Members, acolytes and wannabes are known to have desecrated places of worship and performed lewd acts in public. Yet Pussy Riot are the West's It Girls.

The Orwellian world we inhabit and its IT girls and "girly boys"—the rulers, cultural and political—put a premium on the sameness and uniformity of thought. Their subliminal message, conveyed through the intellectual means of production is this:

Let the peons act out in self-destructive, libertine ways. Mired in—and immobilized by—weenie rebellion, the people are kept from arriving at The Real Revolution: Timeless, immutable truths about human nature and human action.

In the service of sameness, the man-vs.-female biological imperatives are rapidly, if reflexively, being dissolved.

Survival—of the species of the culture of the faith—has a biological dimension. What would have befallen our Hominid ancestors had they implemented gender parity in their hunter-gatherer societies—sometimes the women hunt while the men forage and mind the kids, and vice versa?

Indeed, a reflexive respect for biology has helped Homo sapiens to endure and not go extinct.

A subservient effete civilization will not survive.

In some respect, the 2016 election is about the inevitability of certain eternal verities and their endurance—"not 'blood and soil' tribalism on one side, and not neoconservative propositionalism on the other," as the late Lawrence Auster averred. But a "true and proper love of one's nation, one's country, one's people."

Biology is another of these timeless truths—not biological reductionism, but, rather, biological realism.

Only time will tell whether Trump, a man unsuited to obedience—"a masculine force at full tilt"—will fight for these eternal verities, or be forced into sameness and the sublimation of maleness.

For now, it's safe to say Donald J. Trump is breaking stuff that needs breaking. For our part, we'll have to be grateful for small mercies.

~April 22, 2016

CLOSING ARGUMENT: THE POWER TOOLS OF AN ILLIBERAL POLITICS

Donald Trump's quixotic quest is as much against the malfunctioning media as it is in opposition to the political class. Even as they document their own monumental failures, the wrong-all-the time media continue to practice "wish-fulfillment" (Chapter 18). This persistent pathology of "satisfying a desire through an involuntary thought process" was captured in a February 24 column by Ann Coulter. The commentator picked two "Republican strategists" at random. She then culled a sample of their predictions over seven months. I've chosen the oldest and the newest from each.

On July 26, 2015, Republican strategist Sara Fagen said this on NBC's *Meet the Press*:

"At the end of the day, (Trump) is not going to be the Republican nominee."

The same character, the same forum, said the following on January 3, 2016: "As this field continues to narrow and it's Donald Trump versus one or two other candidates, that's when this race will really come into focus. ... After Iowa, this thing is going to jumble again. ... Christie to me is one that I would watch."

On August 7, 2015, Republican strategist Alex Castellanos waxed fat in CNN's *Newsroom*, about the "Megyn

Kelly moment." Apparently it "killed Trump's opportunity for growth":

> The fire that is Donald Trump is now contained. It's not going anywhere. He is not growing. He was just going to hang on to that white-hot core. His numbers may dip or rise a tiny bit. He is no longer a huge threat to dominate and control the Republican Party.

Castellanos of the overblown phrases surfaces again on another venue (ABC's *This Week*), on December 6, 2015:

> Marco Rubio is the future of the Republican Party, a different Republican Party, if there's a little shot that if this is a Trump-Rubio race, we could see the beginning of a better Republican … But it's not about issues with Trump.

Behind the scenes, strategist Castellanos was running interference under the guise of a group called "ProtectUS," presumably from Trump.

Mentioned in my Opening Statement was a group of shady Republican Party apparatchiks that had convened, late in 2015, in Los Angeles, to subvert the Trump momentum. They were back with a vengeance, mid-February, 2016, this time in Washington. Along for the ride was George W. Bush's henchman, Karl Rove, who, as the *New York Times* reported on February 27 was warning "that Donald J.

Trump's increasingly likely nomination would be catastrophic, dooming the party in November."

Fresh from his victory in South Carolina, Mr. Trump flayed "the Karl Roves and Steven Hayeses," telling Fox News' Chris Wallace: "If you want to keep people like that, characters that can't get themselves arrested, you're never going to win. You're never going win."

Back at the Willard Hotel, Karl's confederacy of knaves reconvened to float plans to "overtake Mr. Trump in a brokered convention." As it transpired, Senate majority leader Mitch McConnell of Kentucky had "laid out a plan that would have lawmakers break with Mr. Trump explicitly in a general election." The party was also thinking of uniting behind a single candidate, not Trump, naturally. The Koch brothers, "the country's most prolific conservative donors," as always, were on the sidelines scheming. Against the Mormon Church's teachings, Republican elder Mitt Romney had taken to spreading rumors about Mr. Trump's allegedly dodgy tax returns. For his part, Mr. Rubio had made some condescending calls to former rivals, his elders, but had been swatted like a Florida house fly for his opportunistic, *chutzpadik* overtures.

Most telling: By the time I reached the end of the *New York Times* story, just cited, about "the Republican Party's Desperate Mission to Stop Donald Trump"—Paul R. LePage of Maine, who stood with Rove in my *previous paragraph*, had endorsed Mr. Trump. To follow were endorsements more major from Senator Jeff Sessions, former Arizona Governor Jan Brewer, Sarah Palin, Kansas

Secretary of State Kris Kobach, former Vice President Dick Cheney, 1996 Republican nominee Bob Dole, and of course, *Duck Dynasty's* Willie Robertson.

And by the time I completed writing the paragraph you've just read, another conclave of political eunuchs had convened to hatch still another plot to unseat Mr. Trump, this time with a Cruz-Kasich unity ticket. Date: March 17. Place: the Army Navy Club, Washington D.C. Duly, desperado Ted Cruz briefly flirted with John Kasich—the Dr. Phil of politics—only to jump from that frying pan into the fire with Carly Fiorina. That farce went on the road and Carly was soon serenading the Cruz kids on their brief trail of tears (unless the footage of crooner Carly on national TV is from The Onion archives). The malfunctioning media develop strange memes, one being that the fleeting Cruz-Kasich alliance was "way too late." That alliance, however, like the one with crooner Carly, was lame, not late.

Since Donald Trump announced for president, establishment troglodytes have busied themselves with predictions of his demise, notwithstanding powerful evidence to the contrary. "He could implode. In Trump's world, the runner-up is a loser": These were the prevailing sentiments heard daily, sometimes hourly—sentiments, for they weren't anchored in reality.

Through "rules changes, subterfuge and faithless delegates, party elites began looking to swindle [Trump] out of the nomination" (Chapter 26). If they so do, warned Pat Buchanan, on April 5, "do they think that the millions who came out to vote for Trump will go home and say: 'We lost it fair and square'?"

Although unwilling to expiate for their deficiencies or make way for those with a record of reliable predictions, members of the charmed circles, nevertheless, surfaced everywhere on TV and radio like rattlesnakes after winter hibernation. These relentlessly dull writers now consider that they've discharged their obligation to news consumers by developing a genre of writing to document their "conspicuous pageant of wrongness," as the *New Yorker's* Evan Osnos put it.

> Trump has been catnip for predictors declaring his imminent political collapse; his candidacy has reached the 'beginning of the end,' or some other description of demise, no fewer than thirty-three times in publications that span the ideological spectrum, according to a tally by ThinkProgress. While liberals might be expected to have misunderstood Trump's appeal, they have not done worse than Republicans such as Charles Krauthammer, of Fox News, who explained, after the first Republican debate, last August, that Trump was "lost for most of the debate," and concluded, 'The real story is the collapse of Trump.'

Confessed Osnos: "[I]n the last few months, a wise editor has twice removed [my own] declarations, in one piece or another, that Trump has reached the beginning of the end."

Belatedly, *Time* magazine had allowed itself to be dragged kicking and screaming by ordinary Americans into the here-and-now. Stated David Von Drehle, in the January 18 issue, "How Trump Won": "There is a reason most presidential candidates stump through diners and living rooms this time of year. They can't fill bigger rooms." To make up for lost reportorial time, *Time's* Drehle went on to describe a revolution that saw thousands standing "for hours in stinging chill to pack an entire sports arena for Trump, and when that venue was full, the overflow spilled into a second megaspace nearby."

In Biloxi, Mississippi.

In Council Bluffs, Iowa.

In Lowell, Massachusetts.

On the Vermont-New Hampshire border.

In Bentonville, Arkansas.

In Madison, Alabama.

On and on, until the Indiana primary, where the first phase of Trump's quixotic quest ended in victory.

To contrast with the "crown princes of Republican politics"—they "can't mount so much as a two-car parade"—"Trump [was] drawing the biggest crowds by far," "has the largest social-media footprint" by far, and "lodges the sharpest attacks on Hillary Clinton, while attracting the greatest number of potential recruits to Republican ranks."

Time's Buy Direct Revolution

Time being *Time*, its writers escaped conclusions about the substantive issues propelling the enthusiasm for Trump—immigration and the systemic failures and sheer foulness of the political class—by laying Trump's popularity at the feet of … yes, technology and celebrity.

The *lumpenproletariat* wants a piece of the famous. The Little People want to become one with their celebrity candidate. The same masses, struggling for their daily bread, want nothing more than to join in a "virtual community." By dumping the political middlemen, "disintermediation," in *Time's* tony nomenclature, Trump voters have come closer to sharing in the "Trumpiverse." *Time's* trendy writers think of the Trump revolution as a Buy Direct, consumer conniption. Shallow folderol, of course, dispelled by many a typical Trumpster interviewed by the Timesters themselves:

> 'It's like this,' says an Army vet called Casady. 'We're going with this guy sink or swim, and we're not going to change our views. It doesn't matter. It's time for us to do a totally insane thing, because we've lost it all. The times demand it, because nothing else is working.'

The so-called Trump Buy Direct Revolution has appeal among groups as disparate as the "anti-war group Code Pink." It praised Trump after the Republican debate in

South Carolina, on February 13. Yet, as Chris Hayes offered effusive praise for the graciousness of his pro-Trump interviewees; the MSNBC anchor, nevertheless, put the typical tartlet to work on tarnishing "these people."

"What defines these people," lisped the prototype journo-girl affectatiously—she had cut her journalistic teeth by going public with a salacious tell-all starring herself as perspicacious Democratic intern to the Anthony Weiner worm—is that "they don't like politicians because of the way [politicians] speak. Trump talks at a lower level. That's what *these people* like about him."

What Mr. Hayes had discovered about "The Trump Coalition" in the course of his investigation contradicted Ubiquitous Strumpet's observations. Here's what Hayes heard again and again:

'I like businessmen.'
'I like bold.'
'He might just fix things in D.C.'
'I voted for Obama twice.'

What a firm grip do Hayes, his hussy guest and the rest have on this complex and oddly marvelous uprising!

No To Neoconservatism

As part of mainstream media, what Chris Hayes peddles never quite rises above a display of pique unmoored from reality. The same level of pastiche is maintained in the reporting on the geopolitics of the Middle East, in general, the invasions of Iraq and Libya, in particular, ongoing in the revisionism underway regarding the genesis of the Islamic State. No, Bernie Sanders (on the Left), the ISIS army isn't comprised of farmers frustrated by climate change. And no, Chucky K, Lindsey Graham and Sean Hannity (on the Right), Iraq did not unravel because Barack Obama failed to complete what his predecessor began. As Mr. Trump (and this writer) had pointed out from the inception, Bush 43's invasion of Iraq, in 2003, was what turned a rogue state into a failed state, giving rise to the murderous Islamic State.

Hindsight about the invasion of Iraq has certainly galvanized the country around Trump. Americans are agreed: Making America great means exposing the misdeeds of George W. Bush with the purpose of not repeating them.

And for a reason.

Bush's domestic and foreign policy bore the birthmarks—nay, the pockmarks—of neoconservatism. September 11 could have just as well resulted in a circling of the wagons at home, as Mr. Trump, by and large, recommends. But such prudence would have contravened the handbook of neoconservatism (available for free at National Review Online). Instead, defending the homeland, Bush translated into bringing about "the triumph of democracy and tolerance in Iraq, in Afghanistan and beyond," as he proclaimed in one of his Addresses to the Nation. This was in keeping with the neo-Jacobin alien persuasion which Irving Kristol—father of neoconservatism and author of *Neoconservatism: The Autobiography of an Idea*— had credited Bush II and his administration with reviving.

While neoconservatives claim—even believe—they are making "the very idea of political conservatism more acceptable to a majority of American voters," their impetus consists in marketing a bastardized idea of American conservatism. Where they haven't already converted people to liberal multiculturalism, pluralism and carefully crafted globalism; their election strategy has been to alienate the natural Republican core constituency in favor of courting powerful, well-heeled minorities.

The ousted core constituency has coalesced around Trump.

As of May 7, the outgoing neoconservative priestly cast had raised its game. Since Donald Trump had effectively clinched the Republican Party's nomination, based on his America First platform, they had an ultimatum for him: Stop your nonsense and we'll take you back. If Trump quit denouncing George Bush and his Good War, and started blaming *only* Barack Obama for Iraq—said commentator-cum-soldier-cum-global crusader Pete Hegseth to an exultant Gretchen Carlson at the Fox News Channel—all would be forgiven. Recall, Trump called Bush a liar and went on to win South Carolina ... and Nevada (Chapter 20). He continues to denounce the "made by Bush" Iraq war. Now that Trump won the nomination, the losing neocons were insisting he get real, renounce the winning plank and perjure himself to The People.

Well, of course. To the losers belong the spoils.

As if on cue, following the deciding Indiana primary, Fox News broadcaster Sean Hannity began beating on breast, begging Trump to hire failed candidates—the kind the country was fleeing. Some of the candidates offered-up by Hannity for his Party healing circle: Governor Bobby Jindal of Louisiana, the man who had scolded former GOP nominee Mitt Romney, in 2012, for his candid and correct "forty-seven percent" comment. ("There are forty-seven percent of the people who will vote for [president Obama] no matter what ... who are with him, who are dependent upon government, who believe that they are victims, who believe the government has a responsibility to care for them.")

Touted too by Hannity was South Carolina Governor Nikki Haley. This divisive party favorite had chosen last year to excise a part of Southern history: Haley tore down the battle flag of the Army of Northern Virginia from the State House grounds, even though the Confederate flag had never flown over an official Confederate building and "was a battle flag intended to honor the great commander Robert E. Lee."

The most venomous cobra head to rise spitting at Trump was House Speaker Paul Ryan.

Paul Ryan, Another Guy Who Never Built A Thing

"I'm just not ready to back Mr. Trump," Ryan noodled to the networks. "The burden of unifying the party" was Trump's. To get a nod from the Speaker, the "presumptive nominee" would need to "appeal to all Americans in every walk of life, every background, a majority of independents and discerning Democrats." (Much as Mitt Romney did, right, Mr. Ryan?) To which the presumptive nominee responded gallantly: "I am not ready to support Speaker Ryan's agenda. The American people have been treated so badly for so long that it's about time for politicians to put them first!"

Speaker Ryan, who voted for the $1.1 trillion 2016 Omnibus Spending Bill, last December, was demanding Trump show him his conservative credentials. This is as though a guy who never built a thing were to mock a man who has built lots of things. This, too, happened; Obama has mocked Trump's private productive-sector achievements.

With the Republican establishment's death rattle growing raspier by the day, here's what observers need to take away from the Ryan contretemps. Over to Trump:

Paul Ryan said that I inherited something very special, the Republican Party. Wrong, I didn't inherit it; I won it with millions of voters!

How many Americans voted for Speaker Ryan, who represents a mere congressional district in Wisconsin? To the role of Speaker, moreover, Ryan was elected by the House of Representatives, *not* by The People. To be precise, only 236 members of a full House chose Ryan as their speaker. The People have chosen Trump. Millions of them.

The People's voice is not God's voice—no libertarian worth his salt would countenance raw democracy, a dispensation in which majorities overrule the rights of individuals. But in the confrontation between Ryan and Trump, the Force is with The Donald.

Yes To Natural Justice

Trump-touting ordinary Americans have a good sense of right and wrong, viscerally, if not intellectually. Are not the common- and natural-law traditions organic systems of justice that rely on eternal verities accessible to all rational human beings? Yes and yes again.

"Man's nature as well as his ethical goal" implies that certain wisdom is accessible to all. Heraclitus of Ephesus, circa 536-470 BC, was led to "the idea of an eternal norm and harmony, which exists unchangeable ... a fundamental law, a universal reason [that] holds sway." So wrote Heinrich A. Rommen, in explaining man's "inborn notion of right and wrong," in *The Natural Law: A Study in Legal and Social History and Philosophy*.

"By natural law," propounded McClellan, in *Liberty, Order, And Justice,* "We mean those principles which are inherent in man's nature as a rational, moral, and social being, and which cannot be casually ignored." Unlike state-created positive law, natural law in not enacted. Rather, it is a higher law—a system of ethics—knowable through reason, revelation and experience. "Statutory man-made law" is not necessarily just law. "What is legally just, may not be what is naturally just," argued McClellan.

In striving for that quality of eternal wisdom—"Sophia" in Greek—one need not work for *The Atlantic* or *The Weekly Standard,* which will always privilege "what is legally right" over "what is naturally right." If anything, it helps to be an outsider.

"You've done me wrong," America's silent majority seems to be saying to their overlords who art in D.C. Translated for *Time* magazine: No, The People don't want a piece of the "Trumpiverse." *The Trump revolution concerns fundamental things like Islam ("no thanks") and immigration ("much less, please").*

This leads me to posit a thesis invoking a concept developed by one of America's greatest political thinkers, in the estimation of historian Clyde N. Wilson. The concept is that of the concurrent majority.

A Concurrent Majority Rising?

In *A Disquisition on Government*, published in 1851, John C. Calhoun developed the profound idea of "two different modes in which the sense of the community may be taken." The one "regards numbers only." The other invokes an entirely different quality or dimension, over and above the "numbers." "The former of these," Calhoun termed "the numerical or absolute majority;" the latter "the concurrent or constitutional majority." The numerical majority "regards numbers only, and considers the whole community as a unit, having but one common interest throughout." Conversely, the constitutional majority considers "the community as made up of different and conflicting interests, as far as the action of the government is concerned."

"So great is the difference, politically speaking, between the two majorities," cautioned Calhoun, "that they cannot be confounded, without leading to great and fatal errors."

The numerical majority Calhoun associated with the "tendency to oppression and abuse of power." He recommended that "the numerical majority ... be one of the elements of a constitutional democracy;" but advised that "to make it the sole element, in order to perfect the constitution and make the government more popular, is one of the greatest and most fatal of political errors."

As early as 1851, the prescient Calhoun was able to categorically state that "the numerical majority will divide the community ... into two great parties, which will be engaged in perpetual struggles to obtain the control of the government." It was to the concurrent majority that Calhoun looked to for unity and transcendence.

> The concurrent majority, on the other hand, tends to unite the most opposite and conflicting interests, and to blend the whole in one common

attachment to the country. By giving to each interest, or portion, the power of self-protection, all strife and struggle between them for ascendency, is prevented; and, thereby, not only every feeling calculated to weaken the attachment to the whole is suppressed, but the individual and the social feelings are made to unite in one common devotion to country. Each sees and feels that it can best promote its own prosperity by conciliating the goodwill, and promoting the prosperity of the others. And hence, there will be diffused throughout the whole community kind feelings between its different portions; and, instead of antipathy, a rivalry amongst them to promote the interests of each other, as far as this can be done consistently with the interest of all. Under the combined influence of these causes, the interests of each would be merged in the common interests of the whole; and thus, the community would become a unit, by becoming the common center of attachment of all its parts. And hence, instead of faction, strife, and struggle for party ascendency, there would be patriotism, nationality, harmony, and a struggle only for supremacy in promoting the common good of the whole.

Could Donald J. Trump be tapping into our country's still-extant concurrent majority? Could Trump be uniting the American Tower of Babble behind things true and shared? These are economic prosperity, national pride and unity, recognizable neighborhoods—a yen that demands an end to the transformation of neighborhoods through centrally planned, mass immigration—and an end to gratuitous wars.

Given the disparate demographic and identity groups rooting for Trump's flawed, mottled candidacy; it would appear that he may have awakened such a majority.

Different though it is, the concept of the "omnibus candidate," floated by historian David Hackett Fischer, is perhaps a more prosaic expression of Calhoun's concurrent majority. An omnibus campaign is one carefully designed to appeal in all cultural regions. Back in the 1840 and 1848 elections, William Henry Harrison and Zachary Taylor, respectively, proved to be "omnibus candidates," popular across cultural regions.

So far, the establishment's reaction to the Trump revolution comports with "the conduct of elites," described by Hackett Fischer in his towering text, *Albion's Seed: Four British Folkways in America*:

> There is a cultural equivalent of the iron law of oligarchy. Small groups dominate every cultural system. They tend to do so by controlling institutions and processes, so that they become the 'governors' of a culture in both a political and mechanical sense.

Explains Hackett Fischer in this magisterial account of American cultural and social origins:

> The iron law of cultural elites is an historical constant, but the relation between elites and other cultural groups is highly variable. Every culture might be seen as a system of bargaining, in which elites maintain their hegemony by concessions to other groups.

These old bargaining processes may have worked in New England's town system, where each community enjoyed a "high degree of autonomy and also a common interest in supporting the system itself." But "reciprocal liberty" in early America's "back settlements" has given way to elite solidarity, hegemony, log-rolling and collusion with favored interests.

In virtue, the American oligarchy currently in control of the intellectual means of production bears no resemblance to the natural aristocracy, the object of Thomas Jefferson's laudable reflections. Likewise, Sir William Berkeley's concept of a society governed by "gentlemen of honor, courage and breeding" is nowhere seen in the fragmented, faction-based politics of America. This is not to say that Donald Trump exemplifies these lost qualities, but, as I hope this volume has conveyed, there's a distinct element of gruff, made-in-America *noblesse oblige* to Trump's political crusade.

Almost 200 years on, Albion's seed is scattered, diluted and demoralized. More so than cultural identities, issues have come to dominate elections.

Nevertheless, in his ability to run strongly in almost every cultural region, Trump is the closest the country has come in a long time to an "omnibus candidate" tapping a "concurrent majority." It remains to be seen how large this concurrent majority awakened truly is. The concurrent majority's success will depend on its ability, and that of the "omnibus candidate," to beat back the sprawling political apparatus that makes up the D.C. Comitatus, now writhing like a fire breathing mythical monster in the throes of death.

Justice's Jaws of Life

Life in the U.S. is still so much better than in the Bernie Sanders approved European dystopia (or in this writer's sad South Africa). Barbaric Britannia is every bit as bad. There, the "Rights of Englishmen," also the inspiration for the American Founders, are dead. In England, a man's right to life is purely nominal. Sundered in the UK is the right to defend that life, a right instantiated in the great system of law that the English people once held dear, including the 1689 English Bill of Rights. These days, an Englishman can be carved up on the streets of Woolwich, yards from the Royal Artillery Barracks, by a "countryman" holding a "different" set of "values." Disarmed Brits and their bobbies—who carry wooden truncheons—may only shoot the savage ... with a camera. (And then upload it to

YouTube, where the homeboy butcher, slick with the blood of an Englishman, is able to carve out for himself a Speakers' Corner, away from the famous, once-so civilized, corner in Hyde Park.)

Inherent in the idea of an inalienable right is the right to mount a vigorous defense of that right. A right that can't be defended is a right in name only. If you cannot by law defend your life, you have no right to life.

That's Europe and the UK. It's not yet the USA.

In September of 2014, a woman at a Vaughan Foods factory, in Moore, Oklahoma, was beheaded by one Alton Nolen, a youthful, hateful black man, convert to Islam, who was terrorizing co-workers into doing the same. Poor Traci Johnson was doing an honest day's work, as Nolen approached her and began sawing at her throat. Suddenly something marvelously American happened. The boss, CEO Mark Vaughan, stopped Nolen in his tracks with a bullet. (What a shame Vaughan didn't stop the butcher *dead* in his tracks.) In the U.S., we still have magnificent men like Mr. Vaughan who're unwilling to relinquish their individual right to arm and proceed against evil. While Mr. Vaughan's right to bear arms is not yet in complete tatters, Dear Leader Obama has issued twenty something new imperial orders against firearm owners and in furtherance of federal tyranny, even suggesting, in a January 2013 White House brief that, "Doctors and other healthcare providers ... need to be able to ask about firearms in their patients' homes and safe storage of those firearms."

Notwithstanding the perennial promises made by those testing presidential waters; it's safe to say that never again will the Bill of Rights be the timeless document of individual liberties in setting limits on government power.

Laws passed in violation of the natural rights of the people, and by altogether skirting the will of the people's representatives, need to be nullified. Trump has recognized that politicians are "chipping away" at the Second Amendment to the Constitution. Should Mr. Trump deliver on his promises, consider nullification his *political power tool*, used by a benevolent Executive to pry the people free.

Nullification should be properly considered as Justice's Jaws of Life.

As I said in the Opening, *in this post-constitutional era, correctives to the corrosive actions of the State will reduce to action and reaction, force and counterforce.*

In the event that he delivers on his promises, does Donald J. Trump possess the "[t]oughness of mind and tenacity of purpose" to buy the country eight years of relative peace and prosperity? To adapt the biblical phrase tethered to the story of Hebrew patriarch Joseph: Should Barack Obama's eight "thin years" be followed by eight "good years"—the stiff-necked American people might just see the error of their former ways.

While libertarians, this writer included, cannot agree with every aspect of the Trump plank; the Right kind of libertarian must at least grasp the following: In a free society, the "vision thing" is left to private individuals; civil servants are kept on a tight leash, because free people understands that a "visionary" bureaucrat is a voracious one and that the grander the government ("great purposes" in Bush babble), the poorer and less free the people.

Donald Trump is no "visionary" vis-à-vis government. If anything, he is practical and pragmatic. He wants a fix for Americans, not a fantasy. A healthy patriotism is associated with Trump's kind of robust particularism—petty provincialism, if you like—and certainly not with the deracinated globalism of the neoconservative and liberal establishment.

The Left calls it fascism; patriots call it nationalism.

Donald Trump has the potential to be just the provincial, America Firster the doctor ordered.

Recrudescence Of An Older Right

Trump's form of nationalism has often been cast by the historically triumphant Left as fascistic. Yet historically, this Right rising has represented broad social strata: It has represented the bourgeoisie—middle-class, liberal and illiberal, standing for professional and commercial interests. It has stood for the working class, the landed aristocracy, the (Catholic) clergy, the military, labor unions, standing as one against the radical Communist or anarchist Left, which promised—and eventually delivered—bloody revolution that destroyed organic, if imperfect, institutions.

This Right, notes Paul Gottfried in his outstanding *Conservatism in America*, appeals to a "deep human attachments and widely held sentiments ... sentiments that are more real to more people than socialist internationalism." Unlike the populist Right, American conservatism-cum-neoconservatism is elitist by nature, and is wedded to propositionalism: The ghastly idea that America is a mere idea—not a community bound by history, ethnicity, language, folklore and common folkways.

While *The Trump Revolution: The Donald's Creative Destruction Deconstructed* casts arguments in the language of natural law and individual rights; it nevertheless aims at what is best for "the little platoon we belong to": our American family. This is the book's "indispensable framework." Simply put, ordered liberty has a cultural and civilizational dimension, stripped of which its constituent parts—our inalienable individual rights and happiness in those rights—cannot and will not endure.

SELECT BIBLIOGRAPHY

Ann Coulter, *Adios, America: The Left's Plan to Turn Our Country Into a Third World Hellhole* (Washington, D.C., 2015).

Clement Wood, *A Complete History of The United States* (Cleveland, Ohio; New York, N.Y, 1941).

Clyde N. Wilson, *The Essential Calhoun* (New Brunswick, New Jersey, 2000).

Cullen Murphy, *Are We Rome? The Fall of An Empire And The Fate of America* (Boston, New York, 2007).

David Hackett Fischer, *Albion's Seed: Four British Folkways in America* (New York, N. Y., 1989).

David N. Mayer, *The Constitutional Thought of Thomas Jefferson* (Virginia, United States, 1994).

Edmund Burke, *Reflections on the Revolution in France* (Oxford World's Classics, 2009, place unavailable).

Felix Morley, *Freedom and Federalism* (Indianapolis, Indiana, 1981).

Select Bibliography

Frank Chodorov, *The Income Tax: Root of All Evil* (New York, 1954).

Jack Kerwick, "Reasons For Trump," Beliefnet.com., February 12, 2016.

Heinrich A. Rommen, *The Natural Law: A Study In Legal And Social History And Philosophy* (Indianapolis, Indiana, 1998).

Hans-Hermann Hoppe, "A Realistic Libertarianism," LewRockwell.com., September 30, 2014.

Ilana Mercer, "A Modest Libertarian Proposal: Keep Jihadis OUT, Not IN," Target Liberty, January 23, 2015.

James McClellan, *Liberty, Order, And Justice: An Introduction to the Constitutional Principles of American Government* (Indianapolis, Indiana, 2000).

John Locke, *Two Treatises of Government* (London, Great Britain, 1993).

Michael Oakeshott, *On History And Other Essays* (Indianapolis, Indiana, 1999).

Murray N. Rothbard, *Power and Market: Government and the Economy* (Kansas, Kansas City, 1970). [Ignore the immigration section other than to consider the bare-bones economics of a global homogeneous world.]

Murray N. Rothbard, *Egalitarianism as a Revolt Against Nature and Other Essays* (Alabama, Auburn, 2000).

Paul Edward Gottfried, *Conservatism in America: Making Sense of the American Right* (New York, N.Y., 2007).

Paul Edward Gottfried, *The Conservative Movement* (New York, N.Y., 1993).

Paul Edward Gottfried, "Russell Kirk—the Conservative Giant That Conservatism Inc. Wants to Forget," The Unz Review, February 7, 2016.

Paul Johnson, *A History of the American People* (New York, N.Y., 1997).

Thomas E. Woods, Jr., *Nullification: How to Resist Federal Tyranny in the 21st Century* (Washington, D.C., 2010).

Thomas E. Woods, Jr., "Nullification: Answering the Objections,"
https://www.libertyclassroom.com/objections/.

INDEX

A

A Disquisition on Government, 226
Abedin, Huma, 180
Absolute majority, 226, 227
Adios America!, 47
Administrative State, 11
Affirmative action, 138
Affordable Care Act, 10
Ailes, Roger, 40, 90, 128, 140, 142
Albright, Madeleine, 189, 191
Alinsky, Saul, 190
Al-Nusra, 175
Al-Qaida, 155, 175
Amanpour, Christiane, 192
America First, 110, 189, 222
American Exceptionalism, 13
American Israel Public Affairs, 38
    AIPAC, 38
Anti-Defamation League, 162
Antiwar.com, iv, 3, 191, 250
Argumentum ad Hitlerum, 188
Arpaio, Joe, 203
Art of The Deal, 44
Assad, Bashar Hafez al, 11, 17, 85, 87, 136, 147, 171

Atlantic, The, 24, 25, 27, 114, 115, 226
Auster, Lawrence, 212

B

Bach, J.S., 184
Baio, Scott, 204
Bash, Dana, 93, 111
Bataclan, 99
Beck, Glenn, 19, 118
Beltway, 14, 37, 50, 88, 127
Benthamite, 179
Berkeley, William, 230
Bill of Rights, 6, 9, 184, 231, 233
Black Lives Matter, 64, 76, 116, 170
Boko Haram, 175
Bourne, Randolph, 106
Brecht, Bertolt, 187
Breitbart News, 35, 80
Brewer, Jan, 215
Brookings Institution, 190
Brown, Gordon, 41
Brown, John, 18
Brussels, 26, 41, 96, 99, 174, 177, 179
Buchanan, Patrick J., 17, 171
Buckley, William F., 13

Bureau of Labor Statistics, 165

Burnham, James, 12

Bush, 49, 81, 84, 91, 110,
118, 135, 138, 146, 148,
149, 151, 154, 156, 162,
221, 222
George, 1, 73, 81, 109,
118, 123, 124, 134, 146,
148, 149, 152, 155, 166,
214, 221, 222
Jeb, 19, 24, 42, 49, 50, 79,
83, 85, 104, 110, 141,
147, 148

Bush Doctrine, 146

C

Caesar, 207

Calhoun, John C., 29, 226

Capitalism, 35, 60, 61, 119,
120

Carlson, Tucker, 34

Carson, Ben, 20, 32, 44, 108

CATO, 165

Center for American Progress,
190

Chafee, Lincoln, 199

Charen, Mona, 19

Cheney, Dick, 91, 110, 216

China, 11, 30, 62, 84, 87,
163, 183, 193

Christie, Chris, 110, 137,
144, 203

Clark, Richard, 154

Classical liberal, 194

Cleveland, Grover, 120, 168

Clinton,
Bill, 22, 64, 134
Chelsey, 199
Hillary, 3, 20, 25, 87, 107,
108, 123, 137, 149, 158,
170, 171, 174, 180, 187,
196, 199, 201, 211, 218

CNN, 23, 24, 31, 47, 49, 67,
68, 71, 72, 76, 78, 80, 88,
91, 93, 107, 109, 111, 127,
152, 155, 157, 181, 191,
192, 201, 205, 211, 213

Coal mines, 116

Code Pink, 149, 219

Concurrent majority, 226

Confederate flag, 223

Conservatism, 13, 16, 150,
234, 238
conservative, iii, 1, 9, 13,
14, 15, 16, 19, 47, 60,
77, 80, 82, 92, 94, 104,
122, 160, 167, 168, 169,
170, 171, 182, 183, 186,
188, 215, 224, 251
conservatives, 12, 14, 15,
16, 17, 82, 119, 160,
167, 168, 169, 170, 181,
183, 187

Constitution, 5, 6, 8, 9, 10,
11, 12, 91, 92, 120, 121,
123, 124, 183, 184, 188,
210, 233

post-constitutional, 1, 5,
   233
Consumption, 87, 164, 165
Cooper, Anderson, 71, 72,
   80, 91, 152, 205
Coulter, Ann, 47, 73, 89,
   138, 145, 172, 173, 213,
   236
Council on Foreign Relations,
   189
Courts, 6, 135
Cowen, Tyler, 23
Cuba, 44
Cultural Marxism, 4, 81
Cupp, S.E., 24, 158, 169

D

Damon, Arwa, 181
Debt, 145, 164, 166
Decalogue, 7, 8
Delegates, 20, 21, 167, 185,
   186, 216
Democracy, 148, 184, 190,
   221, 225, 227, 250
Democratic National
   Committee, 22, 171, 201
DNC, 22
Dogma, 160
Dole, Bob, 216
Dr. Phil, 140, 216
D'Souza, Dinesh, 251
Duke, David, 157, 161

E

Eisenhower, Dwight, 189
Eland, Ivan, 118, 146, 151
Emanuel, Rahm, 106
Emasculation, 209
Equal Protection Clause, 9
Erickson, Erick, 48, 205
Establishment Clause, 7
Europe, 62, 84, 99, 142, 170,
   177, 192, 208, 232
Executive orders, 121, 122
Executive power, 121, 152

F

Farouk, Syed, 104
Federal Reserve Bank, 137,
   164
Federalism, 6, 184
Feminization, 208, 210
Fields, Michelle, 168, 171,
   180, 181, 182
Fiorina, Carly, 88, 110, 216
First Amendment, 7
Fischer, David Hackett, 229,
   236
Foreign policy, 3, 16, 86, 87,
   110, 137, 147, 148, 152,
   177, 189, 190, 191, 193,
   194, 200, 221
Founding Founders, 11, 12,
   185
Fourteenth Amendment, 9

Fox News Channel, 26, 35, 70, 75, 84, 88, 118, 176, 222
FNC, 39, 40, 70, 76, 84, 85, 127
Foxman, Abe, 162
Franklin, Benjamin, 88
Franks, Tommy, 154
Free trade, 162
Freedom House, 190
French Revolution, 16
French, David, 175, 195
Frum, David, 24

G

Gabbard, Tulsi, 171
Gabriel, Brigitte, 177
Gay marriage, 9, 92
Ginsberg, Ben, 185
Goldberg, Jonah, 14, 26, 184
Goldman Sachs, 164
Gottfried, Paul, 13, 15, 18, 234, 238
Government, 1, 2, 3, 4, 5, 6, 7, 8, 9, 17, 19, 34, 36, 39, 47, 57, 63, 85, 86, 87, 92, 96, 119, 120, 121, 122, 124, 135, 160, 164, 165, 168, 177, 184, 189, 194, 223, 227, 233, 234, 251
Graham, Lindsey, 27, 105, 109, 221
Great Depression, v, 166

H

Haley, Nikki, 113, 223
Hannity, Sean, iii, iv, 35, 85, 186, 221, 223
Hardball, 42, 148
Harrison, William Henry, 229
Hayes, Chris, 116, 220
Hayes, Rutherford B., 120
Hayes, Steve, 66
Heritage Foundation, 122, 123
Hitchens, Christopher, 41
Huntington, Samuel P., 178
Hussein, Saddam, 85, 136, 147, 152, 153, 154

I

Immigration, v, 4, 28, 41, 49, 51, 64, 82, 101, 103, 104, 110, 111, 116, 168, 172, 178, 219, 226, 229, 237, 250
Internal Revenue Service, 137
International Atomic Energy Agency (IAEA), 153
International Republican Institute (IRI), 190
Iran, 17, 87, 119, 192
Iraq, iii, v, 17, 23, 44, 69, 81, 85, 91, 93, 118, 136, 138, 146, 147, 148, 149, 151, 153, 154, 155, 156, 171, 200, 221, 222

Index

ISIS, 86, 98, 99, 100, 107, 110, 118, 175, 206, 221
Islamic State, 25, 85, 147, 206, 221
Islam, 4, 28, 101, 108, 109, 112, 170, 174, 175, 176, 177, 178, 179, 207, 226, 232
Israel, 38, 79

J

Jacobs, Jack H., 171
Jaeger, Ralf, 208
Jefferson, Thomas, 6, 92, 176, 230, 236
Jenner, Caitlyn, 202
Jihad, 104, 176
Johnson, Gary, 197
Johnson, Paul, 10
Jones, Van, 157, 158
Judicial review, 7

K

K-1 visa, 101
Kasich, John, 20, 84, 110, 147, 174, 185, 203
Kay, David, 153
Kelly File, 70, 75, 128, 130, 131, 140, 141
Kelly, Megyn, 26, 66, 68, 70, 74, 75, 88, 94, 97, 111, 126, 127, 128, 129, 130,
133, 140, 142, 143, 167, 169, 183, 214
Kerwick, Jack, 12, 159, 237
Keynesian, 164
Kilmeade, Brian, 176
Kirk, Russell, 13, 14, 160, 238
Knockout game, 170
Kobach, Kris, 216
Koch, 26, 27, 67, 90, 94, 95, 215
Koch Brothers, 26, 90, 95
Krauthammer, Charles, 19, 43
Chucky, 19, 43, 167, 221
Kristol, Bill, xii, 195, 198
Kristol, Irving, 221
Ku Klux Klan, 157
KwaZulu, 207

L

Law, 1, 6, 7, 8, 9, 10, 11, 17, 33, 35, 55, 63, 85, 91, 97, 122, 124, 147, 160, 162, 169, 178, 181, 183, 197, 225, 226, 229, 230, 231, 232
Le Pen, Marine, 97, 100
Lee, Robert E., 223
Lemon, Don, 49, 72
Levin, Mark, 1, 60
Lewandowski, Corey, 181
Liberace, 173

Libertarian, v, 1, 4, 21, 29,
    30, 46, 63, 112, 118, 123,
    136, 137, 148, 151, 160,
    163, 164, 185, 225, 233,
    249
Libertarian Party, 197
Libya, 87, 118, 137, 200, 221
Ling, Lisa, 211
Lobbyists, 33, 35, 38, 45, 101
Loesch, Dana, 19
Lowery, Rich, 19

M

Maddow, Rachel, 142, 186
Madison, James, 6
Mainstream Media, 38, 39,
    42, 174, 204, 220
    MSM, 38, 46
Managerial State, 11, 12
Manifest Destiny, 13
Marshall Plan, 136
Martin Luther King Jr., 17, 18
Mason, George, 23, 123
McCain
    John, 27, 53, 55, 58, 87,
        90
    Meghan, 182
McClellan, James, 10, 237
McConnell, Mitch, 122, 215
McElroy, Wendy, 63
Medellín, José, 134
Meyer, David N., 8
Moloch, 191

MSNBC, 23, 67, 116, 127,
    141, 142, 148, 185, 186,
    187, 220
Muhammad, 98, 206, 207
Mukasey, Michael, 19
Multiculturalism, 170
Murdoch, Rupert, 40, 69
Murphy, Cullen, 33, 90
Muslim, 99, 101, 102, 103,
    104, 105, 106, 109, 110,
    111, 135, 147, 149, 160,
    174, 175, 176, 177, 178,
    179, 206, 207, 208, 210

N

National debt, 120, 164, 200
National Democratic Institute
    (NDI), 190
National Journal, 23, 31, 49,
    68
National Review, 12, 13, 14,
    17, 18, 19, 81, 175, 184,
    221
    NRO, 2
Natural law, 5, 124, 225, 235
    natural justice, 225
    positive law, 122, 226
Navarro, Ana, 24, 205
Neoconservatism, 85, 88,
    221, 235
    neoconservative, 13, 14,
        16, 17, 19, 26, 27, 32,
        43, 84, 85, 90, 109,

Index

111, 145, 155, 156, 184, 191, 212, 222, 234

New Deal, 16

New Republic, 155, 195

Newsmax, 40, 140

noblesse oblige, 64, 230

Non-aggression axiom, 112

North Atlantic Treaty Organization, 3, 192
  NATO, 2, 3, 192, 193

North Korea, 62

Nullification, 7, 233
  nullify, 7, 121

NumbersUSA, 173

O

O'Sullivan, John, 18

Oakeshott , Michael, 13, 53, 237

Obama, Barack, 1, 10, 41, 110, 113, 118, 121, 122, 137, 138, 143, 144, 157, 162, 202, 221, 222

Occupy Wall Street, 38, 68

Old Right, 3, 15, 17

O'Malley, Martin, 115, 199

Omnibus candidate, 229, 231

O'Reilly, Bill, 45, 172

P

Palin, Sarah, 118, 215

Parker, Kathleen, 41

Patrick J. Buchanan, iv, 26, 27, 138, 142, 216

Patriotism, 46, 66, 228, 234, 251

Paul, Rand, 69, 85, 87, 109, 111, 118, 126, 136, 137, 139, 148

Paul, Ron, vi, 29, 136, 137, 146, 185, 186

Pavlich, Katie, 19

Perino, Dana, 46, 73

Pfleger, Michael, 207

Plenary power, 112, 123, 178

Political action committee, 38
  super PAC, 31

Political Correctness, 169

Politically incorrect, ii

Politico, 205

Pope Francis, 3

Popperian, 179

Posner, Eric, 178

Postrel, Virginia, 165

Power, Samantha, 200

Presidency, 29, 73, 84, 120, 134, 139, 144, 146, 152

Priebus, Reince, 19, 185, 186

Project for the New American Century, 91

Propositionalism, 212, 235

Pussy Riot, 211

Putin, Vladimir, 45, 85, 147

Q

Qur'an, 175, 176

R

Racism, 158, 159, 169, 170
Raimondo, Justin, iv, 3, 155, 191
Ramos, Jorge, 75
RAND Corporation, 190
Reagan Democrats, 64, 138
Reagan, Ronald, 63, 78, 85, 107, 119, 121, 138
Refugees, 100, 135, 206, 208
Religious Right, 195, 197
Republican National Committee, 4, 19, 107, 150, 185
   GOP, 19, 20, 22, 24, 26, 31, 40, 44, 45, 50, 63, 86, 87, 94, 95, 113, 130, 141, 146, 161, 186, 188, 223
   RNC, 2, 20, 21
Republican Party, 15, 20, 63, 82, 107, 114, 127, 142, 146, 149, 160, 170, 184, 185, 186, 188, 190, 214, 215, 222, 224, 250
Rice, Condoleezza, 153
Rice, Susan, 200
Rights, ii, 5, 6, 7, 14, 47, 85, 92, 120, 122, 123, 124, 125, 179, 184, 194, 225, 233, 235, 251
   inalienable, 194, 232, 235
   individual, 1, 3, 6, 9, 10, 32, 40, 55, 61, 63, 82, 85, 87, 102, 122, 124, 125, 180, 183, 184, 193, 211, 228, 232, 233, 235, 251
   natural, 5, 21, 62, 103, 104, 124, 165, 173, 175, 179, 208, 209, 222, 225, 226, 230, 233, 235
   Rights of Englishmen, 231
Roberts, John G., 10
Robespierre, 16
Rome, 33, 37, 90, 116
Rommen, Heinrich A., 225, 237
Romney, Mitt, 50, 138, 162, 163, 215, 223, 224
Rove, Karl, 214
Rubio, Marco, 17, 84, 90, 109, 111, 113, 114, 137, 141, 144, 147, 179, 203, 214
Rule 40(b), 185
Rumsfeld, Donald, 91, 154
Russia, 11, 17, 84, 86, 87, 108, 119, 147, 183, 193, 249
Ryan, Paul, 90, 91, 92, 94, 160, 223, 224

Index

S

Saint Augustine, 146
Sanders, Bernie, 22, 40, 66,
    76, 116, 119, 147, 171,
    199, 200, 201, 221, 231
Sasse, Ben, 186
Scalia, Antonin, 122, 124
Schanberg, Sydney, 54
Schlafly, Phyllis, 145
Schumer, Chuck, 111, 124
Schwartz, Stephen, 18
Scruton, Roger, 18
Second Amendment, 233
Selma, 158
Sexism, 88, 169
Shahs of Sunset, 192
Silver, Nate, 23
Sobran, Joe, 120
Spencer, Robert, 176
Spooner, Lysander, 6, 63, 155
Stossel, John, 122
Strategist, 42, 88, 148, 205,
    213, 214
Superdelegate, 22
Supremacy Clause, 198
Supreme Court, 6, 122, 124,
    135
Sykes, Charles, 180
Syria, 17, 85, 86, 97, 99, 100,
    110, 118, 136, 137, 181

T

Tapper, Jake, 157
Tax, 8, 32, 37, 46, 62, 119,
    215
Taylor, Zachary, 229
Tea Party, 38
Ted Cruz, 20, 39, 108, 113,
    121, 126, 134, 135, 139,
    149, 167, 193, 202, 216
Tenth Amendment, 6, 7, 8, 9
Testosterone, xii, 209, 210
Time, 24, 75, 92, 171, 218,
    219, 226
Tocqueville, 16
Tower of Babble, 229
Trade, ii, 44, 46, 60, 61, 102,
    107, 162, 163, 165, 166
Transgender, 195
Tripoli Pirates, 176
Tsarnaev brothers, 179
Tubman, Harriet, 18
Tyler, John, 120

U

Unz Review, vi, 13, 54, 56,
    238, 249
Unz, Ron, 56
USSR, 192

V

Values, 15, 16, 101, 104, 106, 119, 151, 159, 160, 182, 231

Vanity Fair, 27, 131

Vatican, 3

Vietnam War, 53, 54

Virginia and Kentucky Resolutions, 6

Virginia Statute for Religious Freedom, 7

Volokh, Eugene, 178

W

Walker, Scott, 82, 84

Wallace, Chris, 70, 156, 215

Walsh, Joan, 41, 67

War On Terror, 176

Ward, Clarissa, 181

Washington Post, 26, 104, 192

Wasserman Schultz, Debbie, 22, 171, 201

Weapons of Mass Destruction (WMD), 153

Webb, James, 63, 138

Weld, Bill, 197

White, Ron, 135

Wilders, Geert, 100

Williamson, Kevin D., 18

Wilson, Clyde N., 226, 236, 251

Winfry, Oprah, 140

Wood, Clement, 91, 236

Woods, Thomas E., 7, 238

Woodward, Bob, 153

Working class, 115, 116, 138, 159

BIOGRAPHICAL NOTE: ON PATRIOTISM

ILANA MERCER is a paleolibertarian writer, author of the pathbreaking *Into The Cannibal's Pot: Lessons for America From Post-Apartheid South Africa,* and columnist for The Unz Review, America's smartest webzine. For fifteen years Ilana penned WND's longest-standing, exclusive, paleolibertarian weekly column, "Return to Reason," which was begun in Canada, circa 1999. Ilana also contributes to the British Libertarian Alliance, to *Quarterly Review* (the celebrated British journal founded in 1809 by Walter Scott, Robert Southey and George Canning), where she is contributing editor, and to Praag, devoted to Afrikaner self-determination. For years, Ilana's "Paleolibertarian Column" was a regular feature on the Russia Today website and in *Junge Freiheit*, a German weekly of excellence. Ilana's online homes are www.ilanamercer.com and www.barelyablog.com.

Ilana has written for *The Financial Post*, *The Globe and Mail* (Canada's national newspapers), *The Vancouver Sun*, *The Report Newsmagazine*, London's *Jewish Chronicle*, *The American Spectator*, *The American Conservative*, and *The New Individualist*. Her work has appeared in *The Calgary Herald*, *The Ottawa Citizen*, *The Orange County Register*, *The Colorado Gazette*, and in other newspapers across the U.S., including *The Valley Morning Star*, *The East Valley Tribune*, *Jacksonville Daily News*,

Washington County News, *Holmes County Register*. Ilana's commentary has also featured on websites such as the Ludwig von Mises Institute, LewRockwell.com, The Hudson Institute, The Association of American Physicians and Surgeons, Laissez Faire City Times, Antiwar.com, FrontPageMagazine.com, Jewcy.com, and Taki's Magazine.

In *Into The Cannibal's Pot: Lessons for America From Post-Apartheid South Africa*, Ilana used the tragic example of post-apartheid South Africa to forewarn Americans of the effects of a shift in their country's founding political dispensation, a shift being achieved stateside through immigration central-planning.

America's political class has been tinkering with the country's historical demographic composition for decades. The consequence of the mass importation of poor, Third World immigrants is that America, like South Africa, is headed to dominant-party status, in which a permanent majority intractably hostile to the host culture consolidates power, and in which voting along racial lines is the rule.

It used to be that the Democratic Party was this nascent majority's political organ, offering a platform of preferential policies for a voting bloc whose "interests are viewed through the prism of racial affiliations." But, as election year 2016 has shown, the Republican Party is vying for a similar mantle. As sure as night follows day, the American democracy is destined to resemble that of South Africa, where a ruling majority party is permanently entrenched, and where voting is characterized by "a muscular mobilization of a race-based community," with a marginalized minority consigned to the status of spectator in the political bleachers.

Ilana considers herself a patriot, a patriot of a different kind; a patriot whose allegiance is not to a party, the government of the day, or to its invariably wicked, un-American policies. The patriotism over the pages of *The Trump Revolution* is not for the American State. Contra conservative Dinesh D'Souza, an opposition to the policies of the American State is not synonymous with an opposition to "America." It's possible to disavow every single action taken by the U.S. government and still love the "little platoons" of America, as Edmund Burke described a man's social mainstay—his family, friends, coreligionists, coworkers.

Patriotism is an affinity for members of one's community, flesh and blood, and to the civilization that made this community cohere; it's an understanding of the principles upon which this country was founded—long since sundered by successive administrations, Republican and Democratic. Patriotism commits to a restoration of the republic of private-property rights, individual liberties and radical decentralization.

This is the patriotism the writer espouses and hopes to have conveyed to readers and converted them to.

A great patriot, historian of the South Clyde N. Wilson, has defined a "political thinker" as one whose "arguments are always cast in philosophical terms," and thus "aim at the true and the right and at the long-term best interests of the common-wealth." The author of this volume hopes to have lived up to the mantle.

~ ILANA MERCER, Washington State, USA, June 2016

Made in the USA
Middletown, DE
27 July 2016